THE PROFESSIONAL'S BOOK OF LOVEBIRDS TS-155

Photography: Glen S. Axelrod, Dr. Herbert R. Axelrod, Horst Bielfeld, S. Bischoff, Rebecca Brega, Thomas Brosset, Michael De Freitas, Michael Gilroy, Fred Harris, Barbara Kotlar, Harry V. Lacey, Ron and Val Moat, Horst Mueller, Fritz Prenzel, H. Reinhard, Mervin F. Roberts, Routedale Agency, San Diego Zoo, Vincent S. Serbin, Tony Tilford, Louise Van Der Meid, Norma Veitch, Vogelpark Walsrode, Dr. Matthew M. Vriends. **Art:** Eric Peake, R.A. Vowles.

Distributed in the UNITED STATES by T.F.H. Publications, Inc., One T.F.H. Plaza, Neptune City, NJ 07753; in CANADA to the Pet Trade by H & L Pet Supplies Inc., 27 Kingston Crescent, Kitchener, Ontario N2B 2T6; Rolf C. Hagen Ltd., 3225 Sartelon Street, Montreal 382 Quebec; in CANADA to the Book Trade by Macmillan of Canada (A Division of Canada Publishing Corporation), 164 Commander Boulevard, Agincourt, Ontario M1S 3C7; in ENGLAND by T.F.H. Publications, The Spinney, Parklands, Portsmouth PO7 6AR; in AUSTRALIA AND THE SOUTH PACIFIC by T.F.H. (Australia) Pty. Ltd., Box 149, Brookvale 2100 N.S.W., Australia; in NEW ZEALAND by Ross Haines & Son, Ltd., 82 D Elizabeth Knox Place, Panmure, Auckland, New Zealand; in the PHILIPPINES by Bio-Research, 5 Lippay Street, San Lorenzo Village, Makati Rizal; in SOUTH AFRICA by Multipet Pty. Ltd., Box 235 New Germany, South Africa 3620. Published by T.F.H. Publications, Inc. Manufactured in the United States of America by T.F.H. Publications, Inc.

The Professional's Book of Lovebirds

BY JOHN COBORN

Contents

This page: A masked lovebird *(Agapornis personata).*

Opposite top (left to right): Female Abyssinian lovebird *(Agapornis taranta);* male Madagascar lovebird *(Agapornis cana);* masked lovebird; American pied light green peach-faced lovebird *(Agapornis roseicollis). Opposite bottom (left to right):* Dutch blue peach-faced lovebird; red-faced lovebird *(Agapornis pullaria);* Dutch blue ino peach-faced lovebird; American yellow peach-faced lovebird.

A pair of peach-faced lovebirds *(Agapornis roseicollis).*

Introduction

Lovebirds are popular little birds that continue to provide more and more enjoyment to those who keep and get to know them.

Throughout history, man has gained untold pleasure in keeping living creatures in cages or aviaries, and birds have always had a special place in the hearts of generations of fanciers. With the exception of certain birds of economic importance, domestic poultry for example, the main motives for keeping birds have been either for purely esthetic purposes, or for scientific research. People who keep and breed birds for pleasure are called aviculturists, and it is the dedication of birdkeepers in the past which has brought the science of aviculture to the advanced state in which it is today. Keeping birds in captivity gives one the opportunity to observe them at . close quarters, without the necessity of seeking out the natural habitat and using hides and binoculars. It allows one to enjoy the splendid colors and patterns of their plumage, to be enchanted by their lively calls or songs, and to marvel at the amusing antics or bizarre appearance of various species at any time one desires. If given suitable captive conditions, which resemble or at least substitute the appropriate wild environment, most birds will soon feel at ease and will exhibit themselves at their best.

At what stage in history birds were first kept by man is not easy to pinpoint, but it was probably long before he could write about the fact. There is evidence, however, in ancient documents, on murals and on ornamental items of both the old and the new worlds, to suggest that birdkeeping was an important recreational activity in many early civilizations. The early orientals of China and Japan have left

"Throughout history, man has gained untold pleasure in keeping living creatures in cages or aviaries, and birds have always had a special place in the hearts of generations of fanciers.

One of the reasons for the popularity of lovebirds is that these little parrots come in several species and a wide range of colors.

Hieroglyphics: a system of writing using pictorial characters, usually associated with the ancient Egyptians.

behind a wealth of bird caricatures, depicted on porcelain ornaments, in carvings and on silks, which have survived the ravages of time. From these, it is possible to recognize bird species—even those which were not necessarily native to the countries from which the caricatures originated.

In the hieroglyphics of the ancient Egyptians, there are references to ibis, waterfowl, doves and parrots, while in South America, the Incas were known to have kept and tamed species such as Amazon parrots and macaws. Even in modern times, primitive peoples in various parts of the world keep parrots

Species: a taxonomical group of individuals that have common attributes and are capable of interbreeding; designated by a common name and by a binomial consisting of the name of the genus and a latinized noun or adjective that grammatically agrees with the generic name.

and other birds purely as household pets.

Over the centuries, many species of bird have been domesticated. In this context, domestication means captive breeding over many generations to the extent that captive mutations (or strains) are often substantially different from the original wild stock in size, pattern and color, as well as in temperament. The domestic fowl, or farmyard hen, is thought to have descended from a species of jungle fowl, *Gallus gallus*, and was probably already domesticated in India as long as 5000 years ago. Over the years it has spread, by the hand of man,

A peach-faced lovebird (*Agapornis roseicollis*) on the wing. The peach-faced is the most common lovebird species in captivity.

to all parts of the world. By selective breeding, many varieties have been produced, some of which bear little resemblance to their wild ancestors. Other bird species (ducks and geese, turkeys, pheasants and quail, for example) have also been domesticated, mainly as items for the menu; others, such as racing pigeons, for their sporting qualities. Perhaps surprisingly, a number of bird species have become domesticated purely from the aspect of their suitability as pets. These include

the canary, the budgerigar, the society or Bengalese finch and the cockatiel, all of which are available in numerous varieties of color and form.

Several species of lovebird, the subjects of this book, can be said to be almost domesticated. In particular, the peach-faced lovebird, *Agapornis roseicollis,* is now available in many color varieties and is popular as a cage or aviary bird in many parts of the world. These little parrots are relative newcomers to aviculture—interest in them first developed in the latter half of the

"By selective breeding, many varieties have been produced, some of which bear little resemblance to their wild ancestors."

Fischer's lovebird (*Agapornis fischeri*) is one of the species in which the sexes are difficult to distinguish.

Although they comprise the most popular species, peach-faced lovebirds (*Agapornis roseicollis*) are usually considered the most quarrelsome.

18th century as Africa was opened up by intense European exploration. However, it was not until the end of the following century that significant numbers of these charming little birds found their way into the cages and aviaries of European fanciers. In the last half of the 20th century, lovebird culture became increasingly popular in many parts of the globe, and this is reflected in the variety of mutations available, second in quantity only to those of the budgerigar.

Lovebirds are small members of the bird order Psittaciformes (parrotlike birds) and the eight species currently recognized are all contained in the genus *Agapornis*. All lovebirds are confined, in their natural habitat, to various parts of Africa and some of its offshore islands. The common name of "lovebird" originated due to the fact that pairs of them will sit close together on a perch, preen each other and generally behave in a loving manner. These habits are somewhat misleading, however, as most lovebirds are notoriously aggressive toward other birds and toward non-familiar members of their own species. Therefore, introductions of new birds to existing stock in cages and aviaries must be carried out with the utmost caution. Of the eight species, one of these is

extremely uncommon in the wild and is rarely seen in captivity. Some of the others, however, frequently reach plague proportions in certain areas of their natural range, becoming serious pests to crops. This, unfortunately, necessitates the culling of some species in vast numbers.

While some species, such as the peach-faced, are extremely easy to keep and breed, others are notoriously difficult, even for the most experienced of aviculturists. Beginners are therefore advised to start with the peach-faced in order to gain valuable experience before graduating to the more difficult varieties. In this book, the author attempts to introduce the beginner to lovebirds, whether one intends to keep a single pair in a cage or a colony in a garden aviary. It is also intended as a quick reference to freshen up on a quick snippet of information. The following text supplies all of the information necessary for the beginner to be able to recognize lovebird species, to select and purchase stock, to prepare accommodation and to maintain and breed these charming little parrots. It is hoped that this information will afford the prospective lovebird enthusiast many years of pleasure and lead him into a whole new field of interest.

Beginning lovebird keepers are encouraged to start out with the peach-faced lovebird (*Agapornis roseicollis*).

Peach-faced lovebird (Agapornis roseicollis). *The more information an owner learns about the natural history of his pet, the better his understanding of the animal's behavior will be.*

Lovebird Natural History

In this chapter we are going to have a look at the evolution, classification and biology of birds in general and lovebirds in particular. There may not seem to be an immediate reason for this, but the majority of people who keep animals of one form or another are keen to learn certain background information about their chosen "pets." This information may not be strictly necessary for the successful maintenance and breeding of a species, but it gives one a greater affinity for the animals in one's care and provides a working background for those who wish to discuss their animals with other fanciers.

THE EVOLUTION OF BIRDS

We do not have to start at the dawn of life itself to discuss the evolution of birds; we can begin in the Triassic period, some 225 million years ago, when the land areas of the earth were dominated by invertebrates, amphibians and reptiles. Apart from insects, there were no flying animals at the beginning of this period, and it was the time that the vertebrates were still finding a foothold on the land, all having originally been aquatic creatures. The various creatures at the time fed either upon the invertebrates or on each other; the herbivores (or plant eaters) came later. A great deal of competition (as is still the case today) existed among the different species and the order of the day was "eat or be eaten." The speedier and more agile creatures therefore stood a greater chance of catching prey, or escaping from predators, than the more lethargic ones. Many of the smaller reptile species took to hunting insects and taking refuge in the trees, but it was not long before larger predatory reptiles took to the trees as well so that they could prey upon the

"We do not have to start at the dawn of life itself to discuss the evolution of birds; we can begin in the Triassic period, some 225 million years ago, when the land areas of earth were dominated by invertebrates, amphibians and reptiles."

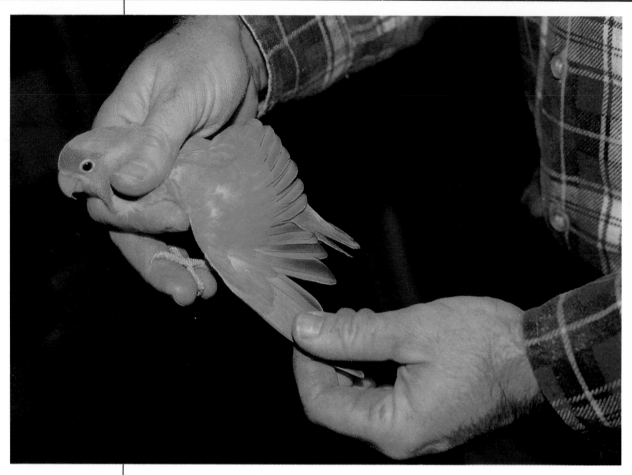

Peach-faced lovebird (*Agapornis roseicollis*). All lovebird species are expert flyers.

"Some 190 million years ago, at the beginning of the Jurassic period, the first flying reptiles appeared."

smaller ones. To escape the predators, the smaller creatures had to become even more agile and speedy and, in turn, the predators themselves had to improve their performances in order to continue to make a living. Those species which did not come up to standard, either in catching prey or escaping predators, soon became extinct, while the survivors continued to develop more efficient ways of staying alive!

These developments, of course, took place over a period of millions of years, and certain creatures began to evolve means of leaping, then gliding, from one tree to the next in order to survive. Some 190 million years ago, at the beginning of the Jurassic period, the first flying reptiles appeared. Known as pterosaurs, which developed from certain primitive lizards,

they were in existence for some 125 million years and, during this period, became the undisputed masters of the air. There were many species, ranging from *Rhamphorhynchus*, with a wingspan of about 60 cm (2 ft), to *Pteranodon*, with a wingspan of 750 cm (25 ft) or more. Perhaps surprisingly, birds did not arise directly from the pterosaurs, but evolved from similar lizardlike ancestors. Birds solved the problems of flight differently from the flying reptiles. Rather than having a membrane of skin spread between the digits, they developed feathers to form flight surfaces and also to insulate the body from the environment. Most birds have very robust hind limbs, which gives them the advantage of being able to move about on the ground as well as to fly in the air. Some, such as waterfowl and gulls, have the ability to move efficiently in three different environments: in the air, on land and in the water—a property not possessed by any other vertebrate (other than modern man!).

The first birds are believed to have appeared in the mid-Jurassic period, about 35 million years after the first pterosaurs and, ironically, were probably largely responsible for the eventual extinction of the flying reptiles some 90 million years later. Our knowledge of primitive birds arises from the study of fossils, and the earliest bird of which there is substantial fossil evidence was *Archaeopteryx.* Found in the Solnhofen

limestone of Bavaria (West Germany), these fossils showed an intermediate form between reptiles and birds. The skeleton was lizardlike but the presence of feathers and wings gave it avian characteristics. Birds radiated to many areas of the earth during the Jurassic period and became adapted to many diverse habitats. Although they were generally smaller in size than their reptilian co-inhabitants, they developed more efficient means of surviving, having a high rate of metabolism and a constant body temperature. They developed complex patterns of behavior, including territorial and courtship displays, nesting, parental care and song. Some

"Some [birds], such as waterfowl and gulls, have the ability to move efficiently in three different environments: in the air, on land and in the water. . ."

Masked lovebird (*Agapornis personata*).

Fischer's lovebird (*Agapornis fischeri*). In the wild, members of this species live in small flocks and are colony breeders.

Vertebrate: members of the subphylum Vertebrata; these members are included in this taxonomical division due to the presence of a spinal column or backbone.

began to undertake long seasonal migrations so that they could benefit from favorable climatic conditions throughout the year.

The progression of the evolution of birds is very scant in the fossil record, and most of our present documentation on the origin of many species is based on comparative studies of other vertebrates laced with a certain amount of logic or theory. It can be safely said, however, that the class Aves became so numerous and successful by the end of the Cretaceous period (about 65 million years ago), that the flying reptiles were no longer able to compete for food and habitat and gradually became extinct. Birds continued to survive, and today they are one of the most numerous classes of the vertebrates.

CLASSIFICATION

There is such an infinite variety of animal and plant species on planet earth that it was almost impossible for scientists to sort one out from the next without a reliable means of classification. During the age of world exploration, which really started in the 15th century, the regular discovery of new species soon had botanists and zoologists tormented by their inability to fit the huge jigsaw puzzle together. At last, in the latter half of the 18th century, Carl von Linne (1707–1788) a Swedish biologist (now generally known as Linnaeus), devised a logical system of classification of plants and animals which, although adapted and improved, is still in use today. His system was called the "binomial system of scientific nomenclature," and in it, every species of plant and animal that is discovered, from a geranium to a giant redwood tree or from a weevil to a whale, is designated with two names. The first name is that of the genus (the generic name); the second, that of the individual species (or trivial name). Taking lovebirds as an example, *Agapornis* is the genus containing all lovebirds, but if we want to specify a particular lovebird species, the red-faced for example, we use the binomial *Agapornis pullari*. Other lovebirds are similarly treated, for example *Agapornis fischeri* (Fischer's lovebird) and *Agapornis cana* (Madagascar lovebird). In addition to the binomial, the name of the first person to describe and name the species, plus the year of the description, may be added. Thus *Agapornis pullaria* (Linnaeus) 1758, tells us that we are dealing specifically with the red-faced lovebird, which was first described by Linnaeus in 1758. As this was the only species of lovebird described by Linnaeus (all others were described many years later) we can assume that, at that time, it was the only species known to European scientists.

What, one may ask, is the point of having these scientific binomials when we have perfectly good English names for the various species? This can perhaps be better understood when we look at the following facts. Animals are called by different names in different languages; in German, for example, lovebirds are known as *Unzertrennliche* (inseparables) and the red-faced lovebird as *Orangekopfchen*. Unless one could speak German, one would not know what this meant. A scientific binomial however, is international and can be understood by any scientist, whether he is German, English,

"During the age of world exploration. . .the regular discovery of new species soon had botanists and zoologists tormented by their inability to fit the huge jigsaw puzzle together."

In the wild, lovebirds do not usually occur in the various color phases seen in captivity, since camouflage is the best way to escape predation.

There are two subspecies of the peach-faced lovebird: *Agapornis roseicollis roseicollis* and *Agapornis roseicollis catumbella*.

"In some species there may be two or more geographical races, which have differences not great enough to warrant specific classification but enough to warrant a subspecies."

Polish or Japanese.

The binomial alone, however, is not sufficient to constitute a general classification. It is further based on a system of rankings, in which the species is the lowest rank and the genus (plural = genera) is the next one up the scale. Species are placed into a genus by a system of similarities of the individual types. Likewise, genera are placed into families, families into orders, orders into classes, and so on up the scale. Should special difficulties arise in the classification of certain groups, intermediate categories such as subfamily or infraorder may be used.

In some species there may be two or more geographical races, which have differences not great

enough to warrant separate specific classification but enough to warrant a subspecies. In such a case, a third name is added to the binomial (thus making it a trinomial) of the species first described, this being simply a repetition of the trivial name, while the new race receives a completely different subspecific name. For example, there are two recognized subspecies of the Madagascar lovebird: *Agapornis cana cana* and *Agapornis cana ablectanea*. The genus, the binomial and the trinomial are usually written in italic script in the printed text, but the higher ranks in the script are usually written in normal type. One of the simplest ways of understanding the system of classification is to study Table 1.

Table 1: Example of Classification of a Lovebird Species

Kingdom	Animalia	All animals
Phylum	Craniata	All chordates
Subphylum	Vertebrata	All vertebrates
Superclass	Tetrapoda	All "limbed" animals
Class	Aves	All birds
Order	Psittaciformes	All parrotlike birds
Family	Psittacidae	All parrots
Subfamily	Psittacinae	Small parrots
Genus	*Agapornis*	Lovebirds
Species	*Agapornis cana*	Madagascar lovebird
Subspecies	*A.c. cana*	Geographical races
	A.c. ablecteana	

Chordate: Animal having some sort of support for the axis of the body and a central nervous system near the back.

The masked lovebird (*Agapornis personata*) is one of the four species that have white orbital rings.

Normal green peach-faced lovebird (*Agapornis roseicollis*); this plumage color is also called the wild color, since it is the color of most peach-faced birds born in the natural habitat.

A normal pied peach-faced lovebird.

BIOLOGY OF BIRDS

A basic knowledge of bird biology can be considered almost essential to the keen aviculturist, whatever kinds of birds he keeps or intends to keep. Birds belong to the class Aves, a group of vertebrates (animals with a backbone) with characteristics which are directly or indirectly related to the power of flight. Although some modern birds, such as penguins or ostriches, lack the power of flight, it can be safely said that all bird ancestors, at some stage or other in their evolution, were able to fly. The skeleton of a bird is made up of strong, but very light, pneumatic bones. Blind-ending extensions of the bronchi (air-supplying canals to the lungs) extend into many parts of the body, including the bones (pneumatic bones), thus making the whole body of the bird very light for its size when compared with a mammal. In addition, the expansion and contraction of these air-sacs, controlled by the actions of the muscles and the movement of wings in flight, ensure a constant and voluminous flow of air over the respiratory surfaces—an important adaptation for animals with a high metabolic rate and energy requirement.

The forelimbs of birds are modified as wings, with three greatly elongated digits (especially the third). In most species the sternum (breastbone) bears a keel, to which the flight muscles are attached. The unique body covering of feathers forms the flight surface and insulates the body against heat loss. The jaws of birds are elongated to form horny beaks, which come in a variety of shapes depending on the

"Although some modern birds, such as penguins or ostriches, lack the power of flight, it can safely be said that all bird ancestors, at some stage or other in their evolution, were able to fly."

Peach-faced lovebird (*Agapornis roseicollis*).

Lovebirds have many features in common with other members of the parrot family while retaining their own special look.

feeding habits of the species; teeth are usually absent. Birds have a four-chambered heart and they are homoiothermic (warm-blooded) in that they are able to maintain the body temperature at a constant level, usually higher than that of the surrounding environment.

There are 27 orders of birds, with an enormous variety of size, form, habit and habitat. The order Psittaciformes, which contains a single family, the Psittacidae, contains all of the 77 genera and approximately 330 species of parrotlike birds. Although having instantly recognizable general features, the parrotlike birds vary in size from the diminutive pigmy parrots *(Micropsitta)*, which at 10 cm (4 in) are smaller than sparrows, to the giant hyacinthine macaw,

Anodorhynchus hyacinthinus, which may attain a length of 100 cm (39 in). Parrot species are found in a variety of habitats throughout the tropical regions of the world.

Most species of parrot are brightly colored, many are highly talented at mimicking the human voice (as well as other sounds), and most are relatively intelligent; these are facts which make them highly desirable as pets. In spite of the differences in size and color, species of parrot have many anatomical features in common. Perhaps the most outstanding characteristic of this group of birds is the beak, which is not unlike that of a bird of prey. A parrot's beak is, however, set higher on the head and is relatively shorter and more curved than that of the raptor. The upper mandible

"Most species of parrot are brightly colored, many are highly talented at mimicking the human voice (as well as other sounds), and most are relatively intelligent. . ."

27

Although Fischer's lovebirds (*Agapornis fischeri*) are difficult to sex, there is a considerable difference in size between the male and the female.

When purchasing a Fischer's lovebird, choose only specimens that have clear, bright colors, as those with dull, washed-out coloration are probably hybrids.

curves down sharply over the lower, and the former is provided with horizontal grooves, which not only help the bird get a better grip of the seeds they feed on but also play a part in keeping the front of the lower bill sharp. The parrot's tongue is large and fleshy and is used to manipulate seed into a convenient position for dehusking or, in some species, to extract pollen and nectar from flowers.

Unlike the members of most avian orders, which have three toes facing forward and one to the rear, parrots share with the order Cuculiformes a unique arrangement of the toes in which the second and third are directed forward, while the first and fourth are directed backward (zygodactylous feet). This gives parrots useful gripping powers which enable them to climb around efficiently among the branches of trees as well as to pick up food items and hold them to their beaks.

The lovebirds are usually placed in the subfamily Psittacinae, although some ornithologists may class them with the pigmy parrots. There are eight recognized species, all of which are predominantly green in color, but there are other colors and differences in pattern which distinguish the species. The total length, from the top of the head to the tip of the tail, varies between 13 and 16 cm (5.25–6.5 in) and most appear to live for at least ten years. They are distributed over most of Africa south of the Sahara, and a single species (with two races) is found on the island of Madagascar (Malagasy Republic). In the wild, they nest in hollow trees, sometimes in termite mounds. While some build just a cushion for the eggs, others build a sophisticated domed nest. In some species, the nest-building female carries nesting materials to the nest site tucked between the feathers of her rump or lower back. The average number of eggs is three to five and the hen normally incubates alone. The incubation period is 20–23 days and the young leave the nest five to six weeks after hatching. The parents continue to feed the young for a while after they leave the nest but, as soon as they are independent, they are driven away. Thus, in captivity, it is important to separate the young from their parents as soon as they are capable of feeding themselves; otherwise, in the close confines of a cage or aviary, serious injury to the fledglings may result.

". . .in captivity, it is important to separate the young from their parents as soon as they are capable of feeding themselves; otherwise, in the close confines of a cage or aviary, serious injury to the fledglings may result."

Fischer's lovebird (*Agapornis fischeri*). Young Fischer's lovebirds have coloration that is much paler than that of adult birds.

Cages and Aviaries for Lovebirds

Opposite: **Peach-faced lovebird** (*Agapornis roseicollis*) **in an indoor aviary.** *This page:* **A pair of heavily pied peach-faced lovebirds.**

Lovebirds are perhaps better suited to aviaries than cages. With a few exceptions, they are naturally nervous birds, and unless a single, very young bird is reared, they do not make the ideal pet. If you have aspirations of teaching your pet lovebird to talk, forget it; although they have very loud and raucous voices, lovebirds' powers of mimicry are almost nil when compared with other parrot species. A pair of lovebirds, however, will make a fine display in a large cage or an indoor aviary, and although they are less likely to become finger tame than a budgie or a cockatiel, they will soon become accustomed to what is going on around them, provided they are not subjected to sudden shocks.

THE DISPLAY CAGE

For those who do not wish to breed lovebirds but want colorful and interesting household pets, a large display cage may be purchased; some very attractive small parrot cages are available on the market. These are usually constructed from stout, chromium plated or stainless steel wire and mounted over a tough plastic base. The wire part of the cage is attached to the base with special clips; this allows easy separation of the parts for cleaning purposes. So that the cage may be suspended

"A pair of lovebirds. . .will make a fine display in a large cage or an indoor aviary, and. . .they will soon become accustomed to what is going on around them. . ."

from a special stand (which may be purchased with the cage) or from a ceiling hook, a ring is usually attached at the top. Alternatively, the cage can simply be placed on a flat surface, such as a table or a sideboard. These cages are available in many sizes and shapes and may be square, rectangular or circular based. The minimum size for a pair of lovebirds should be not less than 50 cm (20 in) in diameter and 70 cm (28 in) tall. The square or rectangular-based cage is preferable, as it gives that extra bit of volume.

Most new cages come complete with all the accessories required to satisfactorily keep a pair of lovebirds. There should be two or more perches set horizontally across the cage at differing heights. They should be placed as far apart as possible so that the birds get maximum exercise in flying from one to the other, but not so close to the bars of the cage that they easily become fouled with droppings. An additional swinging perch is often included, this being suspended by a couple of wires from the roof of the cage. Such a perch provides additional exercise and helps relieve boredom. If possible, it is wise to provide perches of differing thicknesses, thus allowing the birds to exercise the feet and avoid problems such as arthritis or overgrown toenails. Perches are usually manufactured from hardwood or plastic; softwood perches are virtually useless, as the birds will soon whittle these away with their powerful beaks. The best kind of perch is undoubtedly hardwood, as it is more natural than plastic and, although the birds may eventually manage to splinter it up, it will certainly last much longer than softwood and can be fairly easily replaced. To divert their minds from chewing up the perches, the birds may be given a "natural" perch at regular intervals. This consists of a twig from a non-poisonous tree or shrub. If you are unsure about the nature of a certain plant, do not use it. Twigs from fruit trees are the safest (but be sure they have not been treated with insecticides or other chemicals) and they can be jammed across the width of the cage, complete with their leaves, buds and bark. The birds will delight in clambering about them and will soon strip off the leaves and the bark. If they should eat some of

this, all the better, as they will gain valuable trace elements.

Food and water containers, which are made from glass or plastic, are clipped into special spaces between the bars of the cage. They are so designed that they can be easily removed for cleaning and replenishment from outside the cage without frightening the birds. Floor covering may consist of bird sand or floor paper. The former, if purchased from a reliable supplier, should be sterile and contain pieces of grit and trace elements which will aid the birds' digestion. It is also absorbent and will soak up the birds' droppings or any water which is accidentally spilt from the hopper. Floor paper is a kind of sandpaper which is available in sizes to fit the floors of most cages. Advantages of floor paper

"To divert their minds from chewing up the perches, the birds may be given a 'natural' perch at regular intervals."

Lovebirds in a colony breeding aviary—note the nestboxes and the community feeder.

Opposite: Red-faced lovebird (*Agapornis pullaria*). *This page:* A pair of blue masked lovebirds (*Agapornis personata*).

Pied cinnamon peach-faced lovebird (*Agapornis roseicollis*).

"The correct siting of the cage is even more important than the quality of the cage itself, at least as far as the birds' welfare goes."

Pastel blue peach-faced lovebird.

are that it is very easy to change and one does not have the disadvantage of sand scattered by the fluttering of the birds all over the living room floor. Floor coverings should be changed daily and the cage base should be cleaned with soapy water, rinsed and dried. The cage top can be carefully removed from the base, while the birds are sitting on the perches, and placed over a sheet of newspaper on a firm surface while cleaning is in operation.

It may be convenient to allow the birds free flight of the room during cage-cleaning. This will give them some additional exercise and keep them out of the way while you are working. Before letting the birds out of their cage, ensure that all doors and windows are closed and that the chimney is blocked off. Other pets, such as cats or dogs, should obviously not be in the same room when the birds are at liberty. Additionally, you should

secure any valuable ornaments which could be knocked over by the birds and remove houseplants which could be chewed up.

The correct siting of a cage is even more important than the quality of the cage itself, at least as far as the birds' welfare goes. It is advisable to place the cage near a wall, so that members of the family or other pets are unable to move all around it. This gives newly acquired birds in particular a greater sense of security, as they will soon learn that there is a side of the cage from which "danger" is unlikely to approach. The cage should be placed in a draft-free area, but at the same time it should be reasonably ventilated. Although lovebirds are very fond of the sun's rays, the cage should never be placed in a position where it receives direct sunlight for long periods through a glass window, as this can cause rapid overheating and possible heatstroke in the birds. At the same time, lovebirds will appreciate some fresh air, so the cage may be placed in half-shade near an open window or on a veranda when the weather is suitable. Never place a cage directly in front of a working television set, as we do not know if cathode rays can be harmful to the birds. It is a good idea to cover the cage with a light cloth in the evenings after dark so that the birds will get undisturbed rest.

BREEDING CAGES

The best kind of breeding cage for lovebirds is the box-type which is enclosed on all sides except the wire front. The minimum size for such a cage should be 70 cm long x 40 cm deep x 50 cm high (28 x 16 x 20 in). Many pet shops sell unpainted cages, of various sizes, complete with fronts; or one can purchase the wire grilles

separately and construct the rest of the cage oneself, a fairly simple job for the handyperson. Good quality cage fronts are made from chromium plated or stainless steel wire, welded together to form a grille. The grille should have one or two (depending on its size) sliding or hinged doors. The latter, with a secure catch, are probably better for lovebirds, which are clever enough to learn quickly how to open a sliding door. There should also be special gaps in the grille, where water and food hoppers can be affixed.

If constructing one's own cage, one should first ascertain the sizes of cage fronts available so that the cage can be made to the appropriate dimensions. Good quality marine (exterior grade) plywood, about 12 mm (½ in) thick, is probably the best material to use. Carefully work out the sizes for the top, the bottom, the ends and the back (the latter can be made from

Indoor aviaries must have sufficient artificial light, and it is preferable if some indirect sunlight is also available.

"It is best to mount the nestbox on the outside of the cage, so that the birds have more room and it is easier to inspect the box."

undercoat and topcoat of paint. The inside of the cage can be painted with non-toxic emulsion paint, preferably of a light color to give more reflection. As the inside of the cage gets soiled, it is easy to give it a further coat of paint. The outside of the cage may be stained, clear-varnished or given a coat of non-toxic gloss paint. Needless to say, birds should never be introduced to the cage until the paint has thoroughly dried out.

It is best to mount the nestbox on the outside of the cage, so that the birds have more room and it is easier to inspect the box. The birds gain access to the nestbox through a 5 cm (2 in) hole in the wall of the cage. A small perch is affixed to the wall under the hole to give the birds a landing point before entering the nest.

INDOOR AVIARIES

An indoor aviary can be installed or constructed in any part of the house, provided the previously mentioned rules of cage-siting are applied. There are many kinds of indoor aviaries on the market, including an "aviary on wheels" (which is really a very large cage and can easily be moved, say, from the living room onto the balcony on suitable days), or prefabricated aviary panels which can be erected into many shapes and sizes. The most satisfactory kind of indoor aviary is one which is built-in, usually in an alcove or in a spare room. A battery of such aviaries is ideal if breeding is contemplated all the year round (and some lovebirds will persist in breeding in the winter unless the sexes are separated). An advantage of indoor aviaries over outdoor ones is that they do not

thinner and cheaper 6 mm plywood to reduce overall weight). Do not forget to allow for the thicknesses of the wood where the edges overlap; to make things simpler, many do-it-yourself stores have facilities for cutting plywood to size at no extra cost. The timber is simply glued and tacked together to produce a sturdy, boxlike cage to which the wire front is attached with brackets. The grille should be securely attached but easy to remove for cleaning purposes.

A sliding floor tray should be included in the base of the cage, so a space at the bottom of the grille should be left for this facility. The floor tray may be manufactured from thin plywood, sheetmetal or plastic, and it may be possible to purchase these in your pet shop. Whether you buy an unpainted cage or choose to make your own, it is advisable to treat the wood to a good primer,

require a roof (they can go from floor to ceiling) or a shelter. The home do-it-yourselfer can quite easily construct indoor aviaries from 5 x 5 cm (2 x 2 in) timber poles, which are screwed and plugged to the inner walls of the room with the appropriate cross pieces added. Wire netting or weldmesh, to a maximum size of 12 mm x 25 mm (½ x 1 in), can be attached to the *inside* of the framework, covering the timber to prevent the birds from chewing it up.

The aviary door should preferably be no higher than 150 cm (5 ft); as birds tend to fly upwards when disturbed, they are less likely to escape over your head if the door is low-set. Additional safety is acquired by installing a safety porch at the aviary entrance, or in the case of several aviaries, at the door to the room. A single aviary can be made into an extremely attractive feature in the home living area and, although it would be futile to have potted plants inside the aviary, a range of houseplants can be placed around the aviary for decorative effect.

The floor of the indoor aviary can have just plain boards or, preferably, hardboard or thin

"A single aviary can be made into an extremely attractive feature in the home living area. . ."

Peach-faced lovebirds (*Agapornis roseicollis*) in an indoor aviary.

plywood laid to leave as few seams as possible. This will eliminate cracks where disease organisms can multiply, and it will make cleaning operations simpler. At a little extra expense, a plain, good quality vinyl or linoleum floor covering can be placed over the aviary floor, but be sure there are no exposed edges left where the birds could start gnawing with their sharp little beaks. Such a floor can easily be swept and washed with a mild solution of bleach at regular intervals. After the floor has dried, a thin layer of bird sand can be sprinkled over it to stop the adhesion of bird droppings. Indoor aviaries can be of almost any size, but the minimum dimensions for housing a pair of lovebirds should be 150 cm long x 100 cm broad (5 ft x 3 ft) and ceiling height. Aviaries adjoined in batteries should be double wired at the adjoining walls to prevent rival birds from biting each other.

ROOM AVIARIES

A room aviary is similar to an indoor aviary except that the birds have the whole of the room interior to themselves. Such a room aviary is ideal for fanciers who wish to keep those species of lovebirds which will breed on the colony system. To prevent escapes, wire mesh screens should be placed over the windows so that they may be opened for fresh air. It is also advisable to erect a small safety porch at the room entrance. In a room aviary, birds have a greater area to exercise in than they would in a small aviary, and it is easier to clean a whole room than small confined spaces.

"Without doubt, the most suitable kind of accommodation for lovebirds is an outdoor aviary."

Peach-faced lovebirds (*Agapornis roseicollis*). All parrots need perches—both to exercise the muscles of the feet and to help satisfy the urge to gnaw.

OUTDOOR AVIARIES

Without doubt, the most suitable kind of accommodation for lovebirds is an outdoor aviary. The majority of lovebird species are remarkably hardy once they are acclimatized and—providing a dry and draft-proof shelter is available and they receive a good, balanced diet—they may be kept without supplementary heating, even in the most unpleasant temperate winters. However, should temperatures below 5°C (41°F) be expected, it may be wise to install a small heater just large enough to keep the shelter frost-free.

An outdoor aviary consists of a flight, which is exposed to the weather, and an enclosed shelter, which must have adequate windows as birds may refuse to enter a totally dark space. Aviaries may be built in

blocks of two or more, and this is particularly important if selective breeding is contemplated. It may be possible to build flights attached to an existing shed or building, the latter acting as a ready-made shelter which can be modified as necessary. The enclosed part of the shelter can have areas constructed as described for the indoor aviary, leaving a space for one to view the birds and to store food and equipment.

Siting: Having decided to build an aviary in the garden, careful consideration must be given to its siting. One should ensure that no local town planning bylaws are broken and that the aviary is not going to block a neighbor's view, cut out light or cause any other nuisance. Ideally, one should discuss one's ideas with the neighbors at the outset and give reassurance that there will be no nuisance. It is better to get full cooperation from all concerned rather than risk having to remove the aviary later. The aviary should be built in a position which is sheltered from cold, prevailing winds but, at the same time, receives a fair quota of sunlight. An ideal position would be backing onto a south-facing wall (in the northern hemisphere). Alternatively, a dense hedge or a solid back wall to the aviary can be constructed.

The Aviary Base: It is highly desirable to have a short brick or block wall at the base of the aviary and the shelter, if the latter is to be newly constructed. This will give a solid foundation to the aviary and help prevent timber from rotting by keeping it off the ground. In addition, it will stop vermin from burrowing under the edge of the frame and it will make the whole structure look more attractive. The

A pair of immature blue pied peach-faced lovebirds.

"The dimensions of the aviary are a matter of preference and available space, but a suitable minimum floor area for a flight should be about 3 m x 1.5 m (approximately 10 x 5 ft)."

dimension to which the wall is constructed will depend on the size of the aviary; if you intend to purchase pre-fabricated aviary panels, measurements must be exact. If you intend to construct your own panels, however, these can be made to size after the wall is built.

The dimensions of the aviary are a matter of preference and available space, but a suitable minimum floor area for a flight should be about 3 m x 1.5 m (approximately 10 x 5 ft). Try to choose a fairly level area for the aviary and dig a foundation trench to the required dimensions and about 25 cm deep and 25 cm wide (10 x 10 in). Drive wooden pegs into the floor of the trench, and ensure that the top of each peg is level all the way around the trench by using a spirit level and a straight-edge. Prepare concrete (one part cement, two parts sand and four parts gravel mixed with water to a workable consistency) and pour it into the trench until it reaches the tops of the pegs all the way around. Tamp it down with a piece of flat timber until it is reasonably smooth, then allow it to set partially. After four or five hours, scratch the surface of the concrete with the point of a trowel to provide a key for the brickwork. Allow at least 24 hours for the concrete to set before commencing on the wall. This need not be higher than 22.5 cm (9 in) or the height of three standard bricks or a

Peach-faced lovebird (*Agapornis roseicollis*). Note the way the toes grip the perch.

Natural wood perches are great for lovebirds since they provide a source of valuable trace elements. Be sure, however, that the branches you give your birds come only from safe sources and have never been treated with chemicals.

A Nyasa lovebird (*Agapornis lilianae*).

"The timber [for a flight] should be treated with a good quality wood preservative and allowed to dry out before being assembled into frames."

A female Abyssinian lovebird (*Agapornis taranta*). This bird is also known as the black-winged lovebird.

concrete block. Using cement mortar (one part cement to four parts building sand, mixed with water to a workable consistency), construct the brick or block courses, ensuring they are level all the way around by using a spirit level. Upright bolts should be set between the bricks at intervals around the top of the wall; these should be long enough to be firmly cemented into the wall and to pass through the base plates of the flight panels so that they can be bolted into position.

The Flight: At least 48 hours should be allowed for the cement to thoroughly set before attempting to bolt the flight panels into position. Flight panels may be constructed from timber at least 3.75 cm (1½ in) square. The timber should be treated with a good quality wood preservative and allowed to dry out before being assembled into frames. Do not forget to treat the cut areas with preservative before securing joints. The height of the frames should not be less than 1.8 m (6 ft); and this will give an overall height to the aviary of 2.025 m (6 ft 9 in). The most suitable wire to use for the panels is galvanized weldmesh, which is more rigid than wire netting, easier to attach tidily and will not rust. Do not use a mesh size greater than 1.25 x 2.5 cm (½ in x 1 in) or mice will be able to gain entry. The mesh should be attached to the *inside* of the timber, using small, galvanized staples. Ensure that the whole of the inside of the frames (to the edge) is covered with mesh to prevent the birds from chewing at the timber.

Once completed, the frames should be placed in position on the base wall and holes should be drilled in the base plates to fit the upright bolts. After bolting each individual frame to the base, the panels can be joined to each other using more bolts or screws. Finally, the roof panel is fitted; you will probably require some assistance to do this. It is wise to cover the roof and the back walls of the flight, for about one-third of its length from the shelter, with transparent plastic sheeting, so that the birds can

requirements of a shelter are that it be dry and draft-proof. It can be constructed from almost any materials, including timber, brick or blockwork, or aluminum panels. Tongued and grooved cedar boarding is an attractive material which is often used in the construction of garden sheds, bird rooms and aviary shelters; it is easy to work with and alter for individual requirements. Such a

"The two main requirements of a shelter are that it be dry and draft-proof. It can be constructed from almost any materials. . ."

A bevy of blue and normal masked lovebirds (*Agapornis personata*) inside their aviary.

remain outside in inclement weather without adverse effects.

The flight floor may be covered with turf, which can be renewed when it becomes worn or fouled. Alternatively, it can be covered with a 5 cm (2 in) layer of coarse sand, which can be regularly raked over or replaced as necessary. For colonies of lovebirds, a drainable, solid concrete floor will allow regular easy cleaning and hosing down.

The Shelter: The two main

construction should, like the flight, be set on a low foundation wall. It is always best to completely concrete the floor of the shelter, but be sure to include a drain so that the floor can be thoroughly hosed down at regular intervals. With a few modifications, it is possible to construct an aviary shelter from an existing building, or from a pre-fabricated shed or garage.

If an access door is made directly from the shelter into the

A pair of Nyasa lovebirds (*Agapornis lilianae*). It is wise, when purchasing members of this species, to choose birds that have already completed their first molt.

"Adequate windows must be included in the shelter, as lovebirds will not enter a dark area..."

flight, there will be no requirement for a door and a safety porch into the outside part of the flight. The minimum floor area for the shelter (the part confining the birds) should be 1.5 x 1.5 (5 x 5 ft). It is best to include an access corridor at the back or the side of the indoor part of the aviary. This will act as a safety porch, will allow one to view birds and carry out chores in a dry environment, and will serve as a storage area for food and equipment.

Adequate windows must be included in the shelter, as lovebirds will not enter a dark

area (other than a nestbox). Windows to the indoor flight should be protected on the inside with wire-mesh panels, both to stop the birds flying against the glass and injuring themselves, and so that the windows can be opened in suitable weather for fresh air without the birds escaping. Good ventilation is important as, on a hot day, the inside of the shelter can quickly reach high temperatures. In addition to windows, therefore, two or three adjustable air vents should be placed in the walls so that mild ventilation is available, even in

A pair of normal green peach-faced lovebirds (*Agapornis roseicollis*). This color is also known as jade green.

Yellow and white masked lovebirds (*Agapornis personata*).

"The roof of the shelter should be well constructed and the eaves should overlap the walls to protect them during rainy weather."

the winter. Be sure to place the vents in a position where they do not promote drafts directly onto the birds.

The birds will commute between the shelter and the flight by means of a pophole. For lovebirds, this should be about 22.5 x 22.5 cm (9 x 9 in) and situated near the top of the shelter. A sliding door, operated from the outside of the flight by a lever or a chain, will allow you to lock the birds into the shelter at night or to catch birds when necessary. If you should have several aviaries together, it would be very useful to have controllable popholes leading from one enclosure into the next so that birds can be easily manipulated between aviaries if necessary. A small platform situated just below the pophole on either side will help the birds gain access and egress, though they will soon learn to fly straight through the hole without landing. The inside of a timber shelter should be lined with

hardboard or plywood, to prevent drafts coming through the boarding, to increase ventilation and to assist in hygiene. Brick or block shelters should preferably be lined with a smooth rendering. The inside walls can be painted with a light-colored, non-toxic emulsion paint which will encourage cleanliness, reflect illumination and allow one a better view of the birds. The advantage of emulsion paint is that it can be washed and quickly have a new coat applied whenever necessary. This may be done on a warm summer's day, when the birds can be left in the outside flight during painting and drying.

The roof of the shelter should be well constructed and the eaves should overlap the walls to protect them during rainy weather. The roof should slope away from the flight, and it is advisable to have a gutter and a drainpipe to keep rainwater away from the walls. For wooden shelters, bitumen-coated plywood panels covered with a good grade roofing felt are ideal. Brick or block structures may have attractive, tiled roofs.

Perches: Permanent hardwood perches can be affixed across the width of the shelter and the flight. If one is placed at each end of the flight at slightly different heights, the birds will benefit from the exercise provided by the maximum flight distance. Permanent perches should be of varying thicknesses so that the birds get maximum exercise of the feet and keep the claws worn down to a reasonable size. Further perches, in the form of natural boughs from non-poisonous trees, can be placed in the aviary for decoration and for the benefit of the birds, who will delight in stripping off the bark, eating some of it, or using it as nesting material. As such perches become chewed up and untidy looking, they can simply be replaced with fresh ones. Great care should be taken in selecting natural perch material, as certain trees or shrubs (laburnum, yew, oleander, for example) are highly poisonous. To be on the safe side it is best to use the branches of known fruit trees (apple, pear, plum, etc.), but ensure first that these have not been treated with pesticides. Trees such as oak, beech, elder and maple are also safe to use. All branches should be scrubbed and hosed with clean water before being used. Perches should be firmly attached to the aviary structure, using nails or wire, to prevent accidents.

"Great care should be taken in selecting natural perch material, as certain trees or shrubs. . .are highly poisonous."

Peach-faced lovebirds (*Agapornis roseicollis*), normal and American pied light green.

Lovebird Species and Varieties

Opposite and this page: **Red-faced lovebirds (*Agapornis pullaria*). Members of this species often have a hard time adjusting to life in captivity.**

There are eight generally recognized lovebird species, most of which have separate geographical races or domestic mutations (color varieties). In the following text, we will discuss each individual species and its varieties.

RED-FACED LOVEBIRD
  Agapornis pullaria (Linnaeus) 1758
  Synonym: Orange-headed Lovebird
  Now fairly scarce in collections, this species was formerly imported in large numbers. In its

Color mutations: variations which can occur in the wild, albeit rarely, but are most often selectively bred for by man.

Red-faced lovebird (*Agapornis pullaria*). Only one color variety of this species has been documented.

Lutino: a mutation in which melanin is not produced, usually resulting in a yellowish bird; lutino is always recessive.

native habitat it has a wide distribution, ranging from northern Angola and the Gold Coast in the west, eastwards to southwest Ethiopia and the region of Lake Victoria. It mainly inhabits sparsely treed grassland, occurring in small groups of about 20 individuals. Occasionally it reaches plague proportions and may congregate in flocks of 1000 or more, when it becomes a serious agricultural pest and is often culled in large numbers by anxious farmers. The birds are 13–15 cm (5–6 in) in length and they generally feed on seeding grasses near to ground level; they are extremely alert and will speedily depart at the faintest hint of danger.

The red-faced is a little more delicate than most of the other species, and newly imported specimens must be acclimatized with the greatest of care. It is a relatively quiet and peaceful bird and may be kept in colonies with less trouble than one would expect from the more aggressive species. However, its breeding habits are rather different from those of other species and it is classed as a "difficult" captive breeder. In its natural habitat, it normally nests in burrows in termite mounds and, in captivity, it will rarely use a standard lovebird nestbox. However, Arthur Prestwich, the first British breeder of this species, had repeated successes during the mid-1950s, when he provided the birds with barrels laid on their sides and rammed with peat, into which the hens excavated a nest chamber. They are being bred in Europe in increasing numbers and, starting in 1974, Herr Blome of Germany bred and reared numerous individuals over a five-year period. He attributed his successes to the provision of heating pads within the nest chambers, which maintained a temperature of 30°C (86°F) after the chicks had hatched. Red-faced parents are of a nervous disposition and are slow to return to their nests after being disturbed, so the chicks are prone to chills. On hatching, the chicks have a fine, light-reddish down and they fledge at about seven weeks of age. A varied diet should be offered to the adult birds, especially in the breeding season. When rearing chicks, this species will take large numbers of mealworms.

The only documented color variety of this species is, at present, a lutino form, where the green plumage is replaced by yellow. Individuals of this mutation are being bred on the European continent, but can still be considered in relatively short supply.

MADAGASCAR LOVEBIRD
Agapornis cana (Gmelin) 1788
Synonyms: Gray-headed
Lovebird, Lavender-headed
Lovebird

There are two geographical races of the Madagascar lovebird, *A.c. cana* from the north and *A.c. ablecteana* from the southern half of the island of Madagascar (Malagasy Republic). Since the ban of the export of all forms of wildlife from the republic, this species has become rather difficult to obtain but, fortunately, captive breeding programs of existing stock have kept it available, if not abundantly so. In their native habitat, these birds live in thickly

Madagascar lovebirds (*Agapornis cana*), male and female. The color of the male's head provides another name for this species—the gray-headed lovebird.

Female Madagascar lovebird (*Agapornis cana*). This species does not live on the mainland of Africa but on Madagascar and other islands in the Indian Ocean.

"This species seems to have a nervous disposition and regular breeding successes are uncommon."

Male Madagascar lovebird.

normal type nestbox should be provided and should preferably be concealed behind a solid part of the flight framework, so that the birds are not startled each time someone approaches. The hen builds a nest with leaves and strips of bark, which she transports to the nestbox between her rump feathers. The average clutch of four eggs hatches in about 21 days and the young fledge at about five to six weeks. Fledglings must be separated from the parents within a couple of days of leaving the nest—as soon as they are independent—as they will surely be attacked if the parents wish to start another brood.

ABYSSINIAN LOVEBIRD
Agapornis taranta (Stanley) 1814
Synonyms: Black-winged Lovebird, Mountain Parrot
In the wild, two subspecies of the Abyssinian lovebird are recognized, *A. t. taranta* and *A. t. nana*, found in the mountainous

vegetated areas, venturing out into open areas to feed on seeding grasses and sometimes, cultivated crops. The species has been introduced to the Indian Ocean islands of Mauritius, Réunion, Rodriguez, the Seychelles and the Comoros, where it has become a serious agricultural pest. The average length is 13–14 cm (5.25–5.75 in) and the sexes are easy to distinguish, the cock having a pearl gray head, and the hen being uniformly green.

This species seems to have a nervous disposition and regular breeding successes are uncommon. They do not tame readily and usually disappear into their nestboxes at the sight of people, including their keeper. A further problem is that they seem to prefer to nest during the winter months (i.e. November to February in the northern hemisphere); therefore, serious attempts to breed them should be carried out in mildly heated indoor accommodations. A

Abyssinian lovebird (*Agapornis taranta*) taking off. Females of this species lack the red forehead.

In the wild, this species is found in mountainous regions from altitudes of 3000 m (10,000 ft). . .''

Male Abyssinian lovebird.

regions of Ethiopia and adjacent countries. It is one of the larger species, reaching a length of 15.5–16.5 cm (6.25–6.75 in). *A.t. nana* is somewhat smaller than the nominate race. It is easy to distinguish the sexes; the female lacks the red forehead and the red ring around the eye which is characteristic of the male. In the wild, this species is found in mountainous regions from altitudes of 3000 m (10,000 ft), where there is an obviously great range of temperatures (perhaps as much as 30°C or 86°F between day and night readings). These birds are therefore able to tolerate a wide range of temperatures in

This page and opposite: Male Abyssinian lovebirds (*Agapornis taranta*). Members of this species have voices that are softer and more pleasant than those of other lovebirds.

"Abyssinian lovebirds are particularly aggressive and unsuitable for the community aviary; they will bite and break the legs of smaller birds."

captivity, providing they have dry, draft-proof quarters and suitable nesting (roosting) boxes.

Abyssinian lovebirds seem to be relatively scarce in captivity and they have never been imported in great numbers. At the present time, cock birds seem to be in short supply. Successful captive breedings first occurred in Germany in the 1920s and many breedings have since been reported. Apart from feathers plucked from her breast, the female uses little nesting material and will occasionally completely denude her own breast for this purpose. A standard type lovebird nestbox is accepted by this species, and the average clutch size is three to four eggs. The eggs hatch in about 25 days and the hatchlings have a sparse, white downy coat that changes to gray as they grow. They leave the nest at about seven weeks of age.

Abyssinian lovebirds are particularly aggressive and are unsuitable for the community aviary; they will bite and break the legs of smaller birds. They are best kept in single pairs, and offspring should be promptly removed as soon as they are self-supporting. The species is fond of fruit, especially figs (which are said to constitute a large part of their diet in the wild), and some will eagerly take other fruits, including apples, pears and bananas.

The only documented mutation to date is the cinnamon variety, in which the flight feathers are brown, but the secondary flight feathers and underwing coverts remain black. The overall color of the remaining plumage is somewhat lighter than in normal birds. In 1973, a single cock of this type was imported into Britain, and when it was paired with a normal hen, ten cocks were produced, but never any hens. The mode of inheritance of the mutant was never discovered, but as the descendants of these birds are

Eric Peake.

still in British aviaries, there is a good possibility that the variety will reappear in the future.

SWINDERN'S LOVEBIRD

Agapornis swinderniana (Kuhl) 1820
Synonyms: Black-collared Lovebird,
Liberian Lovebird

This species is rarely seen in collections and is considered to be relatively scarce in the wild. The bird was named after a Dutchman, Dr. T. van Swinderen, but an error was made in the original spelling of the scientific name (the last "e" was left out). Under the International Commission on Zoological Nomenclature (ICZN), such an error cannot be corrected unless by international agreement. The average length is about 13 cm (5.25 in). There are three subspecies currently recognized: *A.s. swinderniana* from Liberia, *A.s. zenkeri* from the Cameroons (area between Nigeria and the Republic of Cameroon) and central Zaire, and *A.s. emini* from northeastern Zaire. According to the studies of ornithologists, in the wild habitat these birds rarely descend from the tree tops and their diet consists largely of fruit, especially figs.

Very little has been documented on the captive care of this species, except for a few unreliable reports of specimens kept in their native countries. It seems that unless a large part of their diet consists of figs, they will not thrive. However, examination of the crop contents in wild specimens which have been shot has revealed that considerable amounts of seed and even insects are taken.

PEACH-FACED LOVEBIRD

Agapornis roseicollis (Vieillot) 1817
Synonyms: Rosy-faced Lovebird, Rose-headed Lovebird

This is the most common and best known of the lovebird species. In captivity they are very prolific breeders, and this is reflected in the large number of color varieties which have been produced. They are readily available in Australia due to captive breeding programs, as the import of foreign birds has been banned there for several decades.

There are two documented races, *A.r. roseicollis* from southwest Africa, and *A.r. catumbella* from southern Angola through coastal regions of central Angola. This is the largest of the lovebirds, reaching a length of 17.5 cm (almost 7 in). Originally, the peach-faced was thought to be subspecies of the red-faced *(A. pullaria)* but it was given specific status in 1817. They inhabit fairly arid areas but are rarely far from water supplies. They seem to be the least fussy of lovebirds with regard to nesting sites—they will even take over the nests of weaver birds such as the Mahali weaver, *Plocepasser mahali*, and the sociable weaver, *Philetairus socius*.

The hen bird strips bark from the twigs of living trees and transports the pieces between the feathers of her back and rump to the nest site. Five or six strips at a time may be carried in this way, but if any should be dropped en route, they are not retrieved. Three to five eggs are laid and these hatch in 21–22 days. The hatchlings are covered with a fairly dense coat of

Opposite: Artist's rendering of Swindern's lovebird (Agapornis swinderniana), also known as the black-collared lovebird due to the black band around its neck.

"According to the studies of ornithologists, in the wild habitat these birds rarely descend from the tree tops and their diet consists largely of fruit, especially figs."

reddish down, which is replaced with gray by the tenth day. They leave the nest in five to six weeks. This species can be rather aggressive toward other birds, so they are best kept only with their own species. If intending to keep them on the colony system in an aviary, all birds should be introduced at the same time, and any unpaired birds should be removed as soon as the others have paired up.

Mutations

PASTEL BLUE—Synonyms: Blue, Sea-green, Par-blue.

This variety first appeared in the aviaries of Dutchman P. Habats in 1963. There were two specimens in a nest of five chicks

A pair of normal green peach-faced lovebirds (*Agapornis roseicollis*).

Normal peach-faced lovebird.

"In continental Europe the variety is known as the 'blue'; this is definitely a misnomer, as the birds are in fact greenish-blue, having lost most but not all of the reddish-yellow pigment."

and another hatched from the next clutch of eggs. This is the most popular mutation in Europe, which, bearing in mind its recessive nature, is surprising. In continental Europe the variety is known as the "blue"; this is definitely a misnomer, as the birds are in fact greenish-blue, having lost most but not all of the reddish-yellow pigment. The face is cream rather than white, and the

forehead is darker than the breast. The appearance of the white-faced blues raised much interest when they were produced almost spontaneously by breeders Mallman in Holland and Eyckermann in Belgium in 1977; similar birds also appeared in the USA at about the same time. Mallman obtained his birds from a mating of dark green to pastel blue. These birds still have a faint pinkish tinge on the top of

A lovely pair of Dutch blue peach-faced lovebirds (*Agapornis roseicollis*).

"It was originally thought that the white-faced blue was a distinct variety in its own right, but the current theory is that it is merely a modification of the pastel blue. . ."

Japanese yellow peach-faced lovebirds, also known as cherryheads or golden cherries.

the head and a green suffusion on the back of the head and the wings. It was originally thought that the white-faced blue was a distinct variety in its own right, but the current theory is that it is merely a modification of the pastel blue (such a modification is technically known as an allele).

YELLOW—In 1954 a Japanese breeder, Iwata, produced the first reported yellow mutation of the peach-faced. It became known as the "cherryhead" or "golden cherry" after its reddish face,

lacks the deeper red coloration of the crown as seen on the lutino, and has a turquoise green rump.

The lutino peach-faced lovebird originated in San Diego, California, during 1970 in the aviaries of Mrs. Scherzer. It is a pure yellow bird with a whitish rump and red eyes.

PIED—The pied mutation is thought to have appeared in California as early as the 1930s,

American yellow peach-faced lovebird.

Lutino and normal green peach-faced lovebirds.

which contrasts nicely with the yellow body and the bluish rump. Some of these Japanese birds were introduced into European collections in the late 1960s, Dr. Burkard being one of the first breeders to obtain specimens. The stock did not appear to be very strong, however, and today these birds are not as prolific as one would wish; they remain relatively expensive.

In the USA, a darker form has been developed; some fanciers refer to this as the "American golden cherryhead." It is possible that this is a separate mutation. In Australia, two yellow mutations have appeared. The first type is perhaps confusingly called "cinnamon," when it is in fact deep yellow in color with a tinge of green on the body; the rump is sky blue and there are reddish tinges to the face and tail. In this variety, the young hatch with red eyes, but these darken progressively with age. The second Australian mutation is known as the "yellow" or the "buttercup." It has black eyes,

but it was not until the 1960s that it really came into prominence. There is a possibility that the earlier individuals had a metabolic malfunction which gave them the pied markings, rather than there being a genuine genetic mutation. The distribution of markings on pied birds is very variable and cannot be predicted accurately with a given pair. The present trend is toward selecting individuals which show a predominant ground color (yellow, for example). The pied factor may be combined with other mutations.

DARK FACTOR—This was first bred in the aviaries of Alan Hollingsworth in Australia in 1968 and appears to be very widespread in that country today. The overall green color of the body is replaced by dark olive, the rump is bluish-gray and the flight feathers black. Possessing two dark factors, this variety is called the olive peach-faced lovebird. The dark green, which has only a single dark factor, is intermediate in coloration between the olive and the normal.

CINNAMON—This is a mutation which first appeared in the USA. There is a brownish tinge to the plumage and the overall coloration is slightly paler than in normal birds. The pink facial color is unaffected.

OTHER MUTATIONS—Several other peach-faced mutations are in existence, but the strains are not yet fully developed. Dubious reports of new mutations are frequent, but many of these are a result of metabolic malfunction rather than a genetic mutation and are therefore not carried into further generations. Many peach-faces show varying amounts of red pigment in areas which are normally green. This may be a result of a metabolic malfunction, but it is quite possible that a predominantly red peach-faced may appear in the near future. A recent mutation has arisen in the USA in which the normal pink of the face

Normal green and dark pastel blue peach-faced lovebirds. The dark pastel blue is also known as the cobalt; it is created by crossing a dark factor with a pastel blue.

Cream lutino peach-faced lovebird (*Agapornis roseicollis*). This variety is also known as the Dutch blue ino.

Inbreeding: the act of crossing closely related animals such as fathers and daughters or siblings, concentrating both good and bad genetic traits in the young produced.

Silver cherry peach-faced lovebird. This variety is also known as the American white. It is known as the buttermilk in England and the ivory in Australia.

and breast has been replaced by yellow. Another mutation, known as the gray-wing, has also been reported from America; the basic body color is lime green.

A mutation known as the fallow was developed in West Germany during 1976, while a separate but similar strain is recognized from East Germany. The first chick produced had red eyes and yellowish-green plumage; the feet, like those of the cherryhead, are pink rather than gray.

COLOR COMBINATIONS—It is now possible to produce a wide variety of color combinations by breeding from the basic mutations discussed above.

If a pastel blue peach-faced is paired with a cherryhead, the second generation will give rise to a form known as the "silver cherry." These birds have a pale flush of red on the face, a little darker on the crown; and a pale, creamy plumage with the faintest tinge of blue. In Australia, a similar form, known as the "ivory," is produced using the buttercup instead of the cherryhead.

By pairing a lutino cock with a pastel blue hen, the resulting young will consist of lutino cocks and normal cocks, all split for pastel blue and cream lutino. By mating the offspring brother to sister (or, to avoid inbreeding, by mating a cock and a hen resulting from similar matings) the resulting youngsters will include cream lutinos of both sexes. These birds are red-eyed and have attractive creamy plumage tinged with lemon yellow.

If a pied is mated to a pastel blue and the resulting pied youngsters are mated together, or to another pastel blue, the resulting offspring will be extremely attractive pastel blue pieds with pale yellow and pastel green plumage.

By introducing the dark factor to pastel blues, second generation birds will be dark pastel blues with a cobalt rump. If a double dark factor is used,

70

Normal cinnamon peach-faced lovebird.

Left: **Pied dark pastel blue (or cobalt) peach-faced lovebird (*Agapornis roseicollis*). *Right:* Mauve peach-faced lovebird. This variety is produced by crossing a double dark factor with a pastel blue.**

the resulting birds will be slates with mauve rumps.

Dark factor pieds can be produced by pairing dark factors with pieds and then pairing the resulting youngsters. Dark factor pieds are most attractive, with a strong contrast between the dark olive and yellow markings. Consult Table 2 for a brief summary of expected results from various color matings.

"Dark factor pieds can be produced by pairing dark factors with pieds and then pairing the resulting youngsters. Dark factor pieds are most attractive, with a strong contrast between the dark olive and yellow markings."

Table 2: Summary of expected results from various color matings of peach-faced lovebirds.

COLOR COMBINATION	INITIAL PAIRING (F1)	FINAL PAIRING (F2)
Pied Pastel Blue	Pied x Pastel Blue	Pair resulting Pieds together, or to Pastel Blue
Cream Lutino	Lutino cock x Pastel Blue hen	Pair offspring together
Silver Cherry	Pastel Blue x Cherryhead	Pair offspring together.
Dark Factor Pastel Blue	Olive x Pastel Blue	Pair offspring together to produce both single and double dark factors
Dark Factor Pieds	Olive x Pied	Pair resulting Pieds together or to Olives

Cinnamon slate and cinnamon blue peach-faced lovebirds.

MASKED LOVEBIRD

Agapornis personata
(Reichenow) 1887
Synonyms: Black-masked
Lovebird, Yellow-collared
Lovebird

This and the following three species of lovebird to be described are classed by some taxonomists as related subspecies, with the masked being the nominate race. Although differing in color, they have several features in common, in particular the bare, white-colored circle of skin around the eyes which leads them to being called the "white eye-ringed group." Natural hybridization within the group appears to be scarce but has been recorded; captive hybridization, however, is a fairly regular occurrence, with the result that "impure" birds are often available in the trade. Such hybrids lack the finer points of the pure species and should be avoided if "pure" breeding is contemplated.

The wild habitat of the masked lovebird is in central Tanzania, but a feral population also exists in the region of Dar-es-Salaam. The maximum length is 16 cm (6 in) and the hen is a little larger than the cock. The sexes are very similar except that the white eyering may be slightly more pronounced in the hen (as is the case with all members of the group) and the head is brownish-black, compared with the pure black of the cock.

The masked lovebird is fairly easy to breed, but it is advisable to house them in single pairs and not attempt the colony system. A pair will breed readily in a cage with a minimum length of 90 cm (3 ft); the nestbox should have a width of 12 cm (5 in) and a height of 25 cm (10 in). This species builds a bulky nest, so adequate nesting materials must be provided. Like other members of the group, the average clutch contains three to five eggs which hatch in about 21 days, and the young fledge in five to six weeks.

This species was first bred in 1926 by K. Painter in Ohio, USA, and birds became generally available to aviculturists from 1927 onwards. Breeding successes soon followed in Europe and elsewhere, and the birds proved to be fairly prolific, but not to the extent of the peach-faced.

Mutations

BLUE MASKED—This strain originated from a wild captured bird brought to England in 1927. A further strain was developed in the USA some time later from imported "split" specimens, and birds from this strain have helped to improve the unrelated

Note the striking appearance of this normal masked lovebird.

Some experts classify the lovebirds with white eyerings as races of one species—Agapornis personata—rather than as individual species; these include the masked lovebird (A. personata personata), Fischer's lovebird (A. personata fischeri), the black-cheeked lovebird (A. personata nigrigenis), and the Nyasa lovebird (A. personata lilianae).

British birds. Blue masked are still relatively expensive, as breeders have found that the cocks of this mutation are less vigorous than the hens, with numerous losses occurring during the molt at five to eight months of age.

YELLOW MASKED—A dilute form of the normal, the first yellow masked lovebirds appeared in the USA in 1935. Another mutant, apparently distinct from the American variety, came to the attention of Danish breeder Poul Frandsen in 1964. He managed

"A pure white, individual masked lovebird has been reported just once..."

Blue masked lovebird. Note the light pink bill color, which is much lighter than that of a normal colored bird.

to obtain the original hen and a new strain of yellow masked was developed. There is a considerable variation in the coloration of these birds, some resembling the American type, others being vivid yellow with white primary feathers but retaining the dark mask. The Danish mutants are relatively small, but no doubt the size can be increased by outcrossing with normals.

WHITE MASKED—A pure white, individual masked lovebird has

been reported just once; again, this was in the collection of Danish breeder Poul Frandsen, where it appeared in 1973 in a nest with three normal chicks. It was used for breeding for five years and apparently sired about 20 chicks; but these were all normal, even when it was paired with its own daughters, which should have been split for white. A possible explanation for this is that it was not a true genetic mutation, but that the color was a result of a metabolic defect, which would be non-hereditary.

OTHER MUTATIONS—Pastel blues have been reported from Denmark; these probably descended from hybrids imported from Japan. Birds with a scalloped pattern, somewhat resembling that of the opaline budgerigar but gray rather than black, have also been reported from Denmark.

FISCHER'S LOVEBIRD

Agapornis fischeri (Reichenow) 1887

Found only in a small area of Tanzania, to the south and southeast of Lake Victoria, this species has very similar habits to the masked lovebird. The maximum length is 15 cm (6 in). They were first imported into Europe in 1926 and have since become fairly common in captivity. Once acclimatized, they will breed fairly readily.

Mutations

BLUE—The first blue mutation of the Fischer's lovebird originated in the aviaries of Ronald Horsham in South Africa. Mr. Horsham was really attempting to produce a red form by selecting birds which had the greatest amount of orange on the breast. Three blue youngsters "accidentally" turned

A pair of Fischer's lovebirds. The ground color of this species has the same composition as the peach-faced lovebird.

up in a nest of four. These birds had a blue body and a grayish head but, unfortunately, were not successful in breeding when paired together. Similar separate mutations have appeared in California in 1959 and in 1973. Although all traces of the original mutation seem to have been lost, the most recent strain, at least, seems to be proliferating in American collections.

YELLOW—It is possible that yellow forms of Fischer's lovebirds were developed from masked hybrids, but yellows are currently the most common mutation. A true yellow black-eyed variety has been developed in Australia, but so far has not been very prolific. A few have arrived in Europe and the USA. A lutino form of the Fischer's is also known, but it is still

"It is possible that yellow forms of Fischer's lovebirds were developed from masked hybrids, but yellows are currently the most common mutation."

Yellow Fischer's lovebird (*Agapornis fischeri*).

Artist's rendering of a white or albino Fischer's lovebird. Note the red eye.

extremely rare.

PIED—A small number of pied Fischer's lovebirds are to be found in British and European collections.

OTHER MUTATIONS—Cinnamon and pastel blue mutations have been reported from Switzerland, but these may have been the results of deliberate hybridizations. They did not live for long.

NYASA LOVEBIRD

Agapornis lilianae (Shelley) 1894
Synonyms: Nyasaland Lovebird, Lilians Lovebird, Strawberry Head

Occurring in flocks of 100 or more, usually near water, this species is native to western Malawi, eastern Zambia, and the central and lower Zambesi valley. In spite of its white eyering, this species was confused with the peach-faced when it was first discovered in 1864. It was declared a separate species and named after Miss Lilian Sclater in 1894. They first appeared in Europe in 1926. In 1927, Fr. von Lucanus reported in the magazine *Vögel ferner Länder* (Birds of Far Lands) that a hand-reared specimen was able to repeat the German words: "Na komm, wo bist Du denn?" (Come on, where are you then?) in a hard and hissing tone. This is one of very few reports of a lovebird learning to "talk."

Being generally prolific breeders, it is difficult to understand why they are not common in European collections. As they tend to breed during the winter months, they should be preferably kept in

Nyasa lovebirds (*Agapornis lilianae*). The mask of the Nyasa is lighter than that of the Fischer's lovebird—it is more orange than red.

indoor accommodations. They will breed quite well in the colony system and are best suited to indoor aviaries or bird rooms rather than cages. In the southern hemisphere, they can be kept in outdoor aviaries all year round and are reasonably prominent in Australian and New Zealand collections.

Mutations

The only genuine mutation to date is the lutino, but even these are becoming scarce in recent years. The first lutino was bred in Adelaide, Australia, in 1930, but specimens are currently rare in that country. In 1937, the first lutinos appeared in Europe and a stock was built up by E. Vane in

"In the southern hemisphere, they [Nyasa lovebirds] can be kept in outdoor aviaries all year round and are reasonably prominent in Australian and New Zealand collections."

Yellow or lutino Nyasa lovebird - (*Agapornis lilianae*).

the UK; some of these were exported to Denmark, in 1961, but an outbreak of influenza decimated the strain. In 1940, a separate American strain appeared. There are also reports of a blue mutation from the USA, but this could be a result of hybridization.

BLACK-CHEEKED LOVEBIRD

Agapornis nigrigenis (Sclater) 1906

Synonym: Black-faced Lovebird

This species is similar in habits to the Nyasa lovebird and attains a length of 15.3 cm (6 in). It is found in a small area of southwest Zambia among the northern tributaries of the Zambesi, from Sesheke to the Victoria Falls. This species is not common in captivity, which is surprising, as it is relatively easy to breed. Like other species from the southern hemisphere, they prefer to breed in the northern winter, so are best suited to indoor accommodation. It is sometimes difficult to obtain pure stock, as they have been frequently hybridized with other members of the white eyeringed group. They're perhaps the most docile, friendly and trusting lovebird species and, as such, are the most suitable to keep as household pets.

Mutations

There have been a few reports of mutations, including blues and pieds, but to date there seems to have been little significant progress in the proliferation of new strains.

A pair of black-cheeked lovebirds (*Agapornis nigrigenis*). Members of this species are rather easy-going compared to other lovebirds.

Blue masked lovebird (*Agapornis personata*).

Nutrition

For any animal to remain in peak physical fitness and to maintain its biological functions at an efficient level, it is essential for it to receive a balanced diet. Different birds feed upon various items in the wild, but they always insure that they get sufficient variety of food to provide an intake of the necessary quantities of essential dietary constituents. Taken in the correct ratio, these dietary constituents will ensure that the animal remains healthy. The study of food intake and its effect on the body is known as nutrition. Before considering a suitable diet for captive lovebirds, let us first consider nutrition in general, thus giving us a greater understanding of our birds' food requirements.

DIETARY CONSTITUENTS

Carbohydrates: These are split into three major groups—sugars, starches and cellulose. All carbohydrates are organic compounds of carbon, hydrogen and oxygen in various molecular combinations. The sugars are all sweet to the taste and are water soluble; thus they are the easiest form of carbohydrate to digest. The most common sugar types include glucose, fructose and sucrose. Starches are converted to sugars by the digestive processes so that they are also easily assimilated. Cellulose is indigestible to many animals but is important in adding bulk (fiber) to the diet. Carbohydrates form the largest part of the diet, and they are essential to provide energy and body warmth. Excess

"Different birds feed upon various items in the wild, but they always insure that they get sufficient variety of food to provide an intake of the necessary quantities of essential dietary constituents."

The more
variety your
lovebird gets in
his diet, the
better off he
will be.

*"A deficiency of B
vitamins can cause
diarrhea, poor
appetite,
convulsions, and
wasting muscles;
but, as most seeds
are rich in these
vitamins, a
deficiency is
unlikely in
lovebirds."*

carbohydrates are converted to fats and stored in the tissues.

Fats: Fats are also composed of carbon, hydrogen and oxygen, but have a different molecular structure. All fats are insoluble in water but are assimilated by the digestive processes. They provide energy, help to insulate the body against extremes of temperature, and may also act as shock absorbing material—on the soles of the feet, for example. Excess fat is deposited in the body in the form of adipose tissue and represents a considerable reserve energy source in starvation conditions.

Proteins: These contain the same three basic elements as carbohydrates and fats but, in addition, they contain nitrogen and sometimes sulphur and phosphorus. Proteins are essential constituents of all living cells and are necessary for growth, repair and replacement

of body tissues. They can also provide energy, and excess proteins can be stored as fat.

Vitamins: These are contained in food in minute quantities but are essential for life and health. The most important vitamins are listed below.

VITAMIN A— Also called retinol, this vitamin is essential for efficient growth in juveniles, for adequate eye function and for protection of the mucus membranes. It is found widely in fruit and green foods.

VITAMIN B COMPLEX—There is a considerable number of vitamins in the B complex group, the most important being thiamine, riboflavin and nicotinic acid. A deficiency of B vitamins can cause diarrhea, poor appetite, convulsions and wasting muscles; but, as most seeds are rich in these vitamins, a deficiency is unlikely in lovebirds.

A pair of normal green peach-faced lovebirds—one of them eating an unripe cherry. Keep in mind that anything put into the lovebird cage is fair game for the non-stop gnawing action of these birds. Therefore, everything within reach of the birds must be safe, non-toxic, and not too sharp.

Headstudy of a normal peach-faced lovebird (*Agapornis roseicollis*).

Opposite: A beautiful yellow peach-faced lovebird. Vitamins are essential to the health of the pet lovebird; a lack of certain nutrients will manifest itself in the bird's appearance as well as its overall health.

A variety of feed and water dishes, as well as cages and nestboxes, is available at your local pet shop.

"...[vitamin D] is important in coordinating the function of phosphorus and calcium in the body, important elements in bone building, especially in growing chicks."

A pied edged-white peach-faced lovebird (*Agapornis roseicollis*).

VITAMIN C—A lack of vitamin C (ascorbic acid) in the diet can cause hemorrhage of the mucous membranes and swollen joints. It is found in many foodstuffs but is most abundant in fruit and greenfoods.

VITAMIN D—This vitamin, also known as calciferol, is important in coordinating the function of phosphorus and calcium in the body, important elements in bone building, especially in growing chicks. A deficiency of this vitamin will lead to rickets. Most of the vitamin is manufactured in the body, aided by the effects of sunlight on adult birds, and it is transferred to the embryos through the egg yolk. Sunlight is therefore an important commodity to breeding birds.

VITAMIN E— Also known as tocopherol, this vitamin was first identified as being necessary for the normal fertility of rats. A deficiency can result in various reproductive disorders. It should be assumed that it is important for normal metabolism in lovebirds. It is found in vegetables, fruits and in the germ of many seeds, so a deficiency in lovebirds is unlikely.

VITAMIN K—Found in many green plants and vegetables, this

vitamin is essential to the clotting function of the blood.

Mineral Salts: These, like vitamins, form a small but essential part of a balanced diet. Sometimes referred to as trace elements, mineral salts form the inorganic part of the diet. A great number of different elements in salt form are required for the body to function normally. Mineral salts are required for four main purposes:

1) As constituents of the bones (the rigid structures which support the muscular system of the body), beak, nails and the eggshell. The major minerals in this group include calcium, phosphorus and magnesium.

2) As constituents of the body cells of which muscle, blood corpuscles, liver and so on, are composed. These include iron, sulphur, potassium and phosphorus.

3) As soluble salts which give the body fluids their composition and stability. These include sodium, potassium and chlorine.

4) As factors involved with chemical reactions in the body, especially those concerned with the release of energy during normal metabolism. These include phosphorus, magnesium and iron.

In addition to the more common minerals mentioned above, many others, such as cobalt, copper, iodine, molybdenum and nickel, are required in minute quantities. Fortunately, most of these trace elements are contained in the types of foods commonly available for captive lovebirds.

FOODS AND FEEDING
Although the foregoing information may seem overly complicated, it is not really

"In addition to the more common minerals. . .many others, such as cobalt, copper, iodine, molybdenum and nickel, are required in minute quantities."

Offering your bird (or birds) small portions of different types of food will help determine his particular likes and dislikes.

A pair of blue masked lovebirds (*Agapornis personata*). Always remember that lovebird does not live by seed alone.

difficult to provide lovebirds with a balanced diet containing all of the essential dietary constituents. A mixture of seeds, some greenfood or fruit, and a vitamin/mineral supplement will occasionally provide all they require. The greater part of the diet consists of various seeds, especially canary and millet. Seed mixes for lovebirds can be

breeding pairs are thoroughly equipped for the strenuous task of brooding and rearing the young, and that the youngsters themselves receive adequate protein for development. Outside the breeding season, things are much more relaxed, so a slightly less rich diet is provided, which will help ensure that the birds do not become overweight.

obtained from specialist avicultural suppliers, but it is often more fun (and cheaper) to buy individual seed types in bulk and to make your own mixtures, based on the types of seeds your particular lovebirds show preference for.

Lovebirds can show individual preferences in food intake, and while one bird may be crazy about canary seed, for example, another may only take it in extreme emergency (i.e. when there is nothing else!). The following menus are examples of seed diets to try during the breeding season and during the "resting period." The first is richer in protein and fat than the second, thus ensuring that

"Lovebirds can show individual preferences in food intake, and while one bird may be crazy about canary seed, for example, another may only take it in extreme emergency (i.e. when there is nothing else!)."

Seed mixture for breeding/molting periods
45% millet (of various types)
30% canary seed
15% sunflower seed
5% oats
3% hemp
2% niger seed
Seed mixture for resting period
60% millet (of various types)
20% canary seed
12% sunflower seed
3% oats
3% hemp
2% niger seed
Note: Sunflower seed or hemp should never be given in greater percentages than those indicated above. They are both very high in oil (fat) content and, although

A blue masked lovebird and a yellow masked lovebird.

"Damp seed will develop mold and can have detrimental effects if it is fed to the birds."

the birds like to eat them very much, excessive consumption will lead to obesity and poor breeding results.

Various seed from avicultural stores is usually supplied in sacks or paper or plastic bags. It should not be stored for long in such containers, however, as they are subject to easy entry by rodent or insect pests. Seed should preferably be stored in metal bins (clean, galvanized trash cans are ideal) and, when not in use, the lid should be left tightly closed. This will protect the seed from mouse droppings (which can harbor unpleasant diseases) and keep it dry. Damp seed will develop mold and can have detrimental effects if it is fed to the birds.

The seed should be given to the birds in stainless steel, porcelain or strong plastic dishes or hoppers. The latter are self-filling and only require occasional replenishment, but one should ensure that empty seed husks are regularly

Note the clean, tight plumage on these peach-faced lovebirds (*Agapornis roseicollis*). No bird can look its best without a proper diet.

removed from the feeding surface. This can be done by stirring the surface of the seed and gently blowing away the empty husks. As most birds de-husk the seeds before swallowing the kernel, the husks frequently drop back into the food container, eventually concealing the uneaten food. It is not unknown for birds to have starved, when having an almost full container of food, because their owner failed to remove the empty husks. Open seed containers should be emptied and cleaned out at regular

intervals. Never place them below perches, where they will soon be fouled by the birds' droppings. In an open aviary, it is best to place the seed tray off the ground on a special shelf, under cover to prevent rain wetting the food.

Soaked Seed: Providing soaked bird seed is an excellent

Nyasa lovebirds (*Agapornis lilianae*).

Providing soaked bird seed is an excellent way to vary the diet and increase its nutritional value."

way to vary the diet and increase its nutritional value. If seed is immersed in water for not more than 24 hours (any longer will cause it to ferment), the germinating process begins and chemical changes in the structure produce greater levels of protein. Additionally, the whole seed becomes more easily digestible. Soaked seed is of excellent value during the breeding season, particularly while youngsters are in the nest; the partially digested seed passed to the nestlings by the parent birds will be in a more acceptable and nutritious form. Soaked seed can also be used as a tonic for birds suffering from

Pied edged-yellow peach-faced lovebird (Agapornis roseicollis).

"Most forms of bird seed are suitable for supplying to the birds in soaked form, and one can either soak a seed mixture or soak individual types to be fed on a rotating basis."

Edged-white peach-faced lovebird. This variety is produced by a pastel blue/edged-yellow cross.

stress, or during treatment of or recovery from a disease. However, it should not replace the normal dry seed, but should be offered at regular intervals throughout the year and daily during the breeding season.

Most forms of bird seed are suitable for supplying to the birds in soaked form, and one can either soak a seed mixture or soak individual types to be fed on a rotating basis. The required quantity of seed is placed in a shallow container, and cold (or very slightly lukewarm) water is poured over it until the grains are fully immersed (you may have to stir it about to ensure that all the seed is wet). The container is then put in a warm place (such as an open cupboard) and allowed to stand for 12–24 hours, after which it should be drained through a fine meshed strainer and rinsed thoroughly with clean, cold water. The seed should then be partially dried by tipping it onto a clean, absorbent

towel. It may be served in a shallow dish. Only small amounts of seed at a time should be prepared in this way, as it soon sours, particularly in warm weather. Uneaten soaked seed should be removed at the end of each day and discarded. For reasons of economy, you are advised to assess the amount of soaked seed which can be easily consumed by your birds each day and to prepare no more than that amount.

Millet Sprays: The natural "ears" from the living millet plant are dried out without being thrashed and are then supplied as millet sprays. The removal of seeds from the sprays is a natural method of feeding for the birds—they will derive great pleasure in feeding from them. When sprays are available, birds will often ignore the seed in the dishes and concentrate on the sprays. Millet sprays may be

obtained from your seed supplier and should be given conservatively to your bird (perhaps one spray per pair every other day). If you give them too much, they may eat only the spray and therefore receive an inadequate diet (this is not to say that millet is not a nutritious seed, but variety is important). The spray should be tied high up on the cage wire so that the birds derive some exercise in reaching it.

Greenfood: Fresh greenfood contains certain vitamins which may not be present in seed in sufficient quantities. It is important, therefore, that the lovebird's prime diet of seed is supplemented with a variety of greenfood and fruit. Lettuce is eagerly accepted but, as it has little nutritional value, it should only be given sparingly. Spinach, which can be grown in the garden for most of the year, is more nutritious, containing valuable vitamins and minerals. Wild seeding grasses of various types are universal and it is easy to collect them, tie them in sheafs, and suspend them in the cage or aviary. There are many wild herbs in different parts of the world which can be used as food for lovebirds; in Europe and the USA, chickweed, groundsel and dandelion can be collected. Wherever you are, try to find out what other hobbyists select as wild greenfood for their animals. What is enjoyed by rabbits or chickens is also likely to be suitable for lovebirds.

When collecting wild greenfood, great care must be taken to ensure that there are no poisonous or suspect plants hidden in your bundle. Avoid collecting along roadsides, where plants are likely to be polluted with vehicle fumes or the droppings of domestic animals. In addition, never use anything which is suspected to have been treated with insecticides, fungicides, herbicides, or chemical fertilizers. Twigs from non-poisonous trees or shrubs can be given, and the birds will eat some of the leaves or buds and strip the bark. Most lovebirds will

"Millet sprays may be obtained from your seed supplier and should be given conservatively to your bird. . .If you give them too much, they may eat only the spray and therefore receive an inadequate diet. . ."

Blue masked
lovebirds
(*Agapornis
personata*)

Fischer's
lovebirds
(*Agapornis
fischeri*).

these are used in grinding up the food by the muscular actions of the gizzard walls. The food is ground up into a fluid mass, so that it can pass on through the system while the grit remains in the gizzard. The bird may also gain valuable trace elements from the grit as it is gradually worn down. A bird with no access to grit would be unable to digest its food properly, and this gives rise to problems such as nutritional deficiencies, anemia and constipation. Various grades of grit may be purchased from your pet shop. This may consist of a mixture of crushed stones, crushed seashells and pieces of cuttlefish bone, all of which have been thoroughly washed, sterilized and dried out. Bird sand, supplied for use on cage floors, may also contain a proportion of grit. It is best to supply grit in special shallow containers, separate from the food, so that you may monitor how much of it is being taken. If

Millet spray is a big favorite among most parrots. It is often used as a special treat.

Pet shop dealers can be extremely helpful when it comes to purchasing lovebird necessities.

nibble at fruit or vegetables, and you can try to tempt them regularly with a piece of apple, pear, plum, banana or carrot. Not all birds will take everything you offer them, but it will do no harm to experiment with various fruits and vegetables to see what individual birds prefer. Should the birds get diarrhea at any time, the feeding of fruit and greenfood should be temporarily suspended, at least until the cause of the ailment has been removed.

GRIT AND CUTTLEFISH BONE
A bird's digestive system demands that it has grit in its gizzard. The bird swallows small stones, pieces of gravel and other insoluble materials, and

your birds do not seem to be taking much grit from the supply dish in outdoor aviaries, do not worry, as they will be picking up items from the aviary floor. However, to be on the safe side, supplementary grit should always be available.

One of the most important minerals in the diet is calcium, which is essential for the formation of strong eggshells and bones in growing chicks; it is also important in feather growth, especially during the molt. One of the easiest ways of giving additional calcium to birds is to supply them with cuttlefish bone. This is the internal skeleton of the squidlike cuttlefish and is rich in calcium salts as well as other trace elements. Prepared cuttlefish bones are available from pet shops. They are clipped to the cage wire, and the birds can nibble pieces off as they require them. If you're able to collect your own cuttlefish bones from the seashore, they should first be treated to remove sea salt

and dirt before being given to your birds. To do this, soak them in clean water for 48 hours, leave them under running water for an additional eight hours, then dry them out on clean, absorbent paper or towels and they will be ready for use. Eggshells are also rich in calcium, and those of domestic hens (after you have eaten the contents) may be baked in the oven until they are brittle (but not burnt), then crushed and added to the birds' grit supply.

Most pet shops stock many types of seed and several types of millet.

"One of the most important minerals in the diet is calcium, which is essential for the formation of strong eggshells and bones in growing chicks. . ."

Grit and cuttlebone are important digestive aids for lovebirds; additionally, they provide a major source of calcium.

Water bottles can be purchased with the cage or separately. Always remember that fresh water must be provided daily.

"Vitamin/mineral tonics are particularly effective during the breeding and molting seasons, when the birds' health is under pressure."

Center: Water bottles or dishes must be securely attached to the cage to avoid spillage. *Bottom:* Cuttlebone should be attached in a location convenient to one of the perches so that the lovebirds can scrape away when they feel the need.

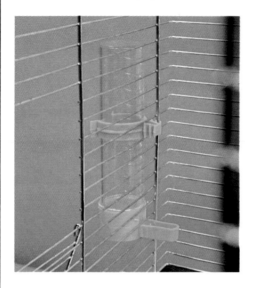

SUPPLEMENTS AND TONICS

Manufacturers of pet foods and requisites are continually bringing out new brands of vitamin and mineral supplements. These vary in quality and effect; it is best to select well-known brands or those with a proven track record—there are plenty to choose from.

Vitamin/mineral tonics are particularly effective during the breeding and molting seasons,

when the birds' health is under pressure. There are supplements in fluid form, which may be added to the drinking water, and others in powder form, which may be mixed in with the seed. Use such tonics as the manufacturer instructs and do *not* be tempted to give overdoses. Too much of a vitamin/mineral supplement can be more dangerous than none at all.

Lovebirds may sometimes be observed eating their own droppings and those of other birds. To human minds, this may seem to be an unpleasant habit, but in the wild many animals do this with a good reason. Certain vitamins of the B complex group, in particular B_2 (riboflavin) and B_{12} (cyanocobalamin), are actually manufactured in the gut of a living animal during the digestive processes. By eating the droppings, the birds are gaining an additional supply of the vitamins. Unfortunately, certain enteric diseases are also transmitted through droppings, so the eating of droppings should be discouraged as much as possible by supplying vitamin/mineral supplements and keeping food containers clear of perches.

WATER

This is not usually classed as part of a diet but, nevertheless, water is an essential commodity. It forms more than 90% of the body tissues of organisms and, as it is being continually lost through evaporation, there must be a facility for it to be replenished at all times. Birds taking regular supplies of greenfood and fruit will not drink as much water as birds taking mainly seed. However, clean, fresh water must always be available to your birds. In cages, the water can be supplied in special pots or water fountains which are clipped to the wire. Whatever form of water container is used, however, the water must be changed and the pot cleaned daily. In the aviary, the water can be supplied in a small "pond." This may be a simple, large, shallow dish, with the water depth not exceeding 2.5 cm (1 in). If the sides of the dish are such that the water can be deeper than this, holes should be drilled at the desired water level so that the shallow depth is maintained should it rain; otherwise one stands the risk of birds drowning. Some birds will use the dish for bathing as well as drinking, so there is not much point in having separate vessels, as the birds will not distinguish between the two.

Above: It is a good idea to purchase your lovebird's basic necessities before you bring him home. *Below:* Normal peach-faced lovebird (*Agapornis roseicollis*).

Peach-faced lovebird (*Agapornis roseicollis*) sitting on the dock of its nestbox. Determining the sex of the peach-faced is difficult; usually the hen is a bit larger than the male and her legs are farther apart.

Breeding Lovebirds

A clutch of masked lovebird (*Agapornis personata*) eggs. The average clutch for this species consists of five eggs.

Most of the lovebird species have been bred in captivity at some time or other, but some tend to be more prolific, thus "easier" than others. A knowledge of the birds' breeding strategies in the wild will go a long way towards success in captive breeding. With the exception of Swindern's lovebird, which has rarely been kept in captivity let alone bred, the most "difficult" species is undoubtedly the red-faced, which in the wild builds its own nesting cavity by burrowing into a termite mound. There is evidence that the high humidity and constant temperatures found in such termite mounds play an important part in the development of the embryos. Varying amounts of success have been achieved by providing captive birds of this species with barrels or boxes rammed full with damp peat, into which the birds can burrow. Most species of lovebird nest in hollow trees or branches, and a good substitute for these in captive conditions is a nestbox.

Without doubt, the easiest species to breed is the peach-faced. It is therefore more readily obtainable than others. It is highly recommended that the beginner to lovebird keeping should gain experience with this species before attempting to breed the rarer and more difficult ones.

SEX DETERMINATION

The first and most important factor, if one intends to breed lovebirds, is the possession of a true pair; in other words, a cock and a hen. To beginners, this is not always as easy as it may seem, and many have kept an

"The first and most important factor, if one intends to breed lovebirds, is the possession of a true pair; in other words, a cock and a hen."

Pied green and Dutch blue peach-faced lovebirds (*Agapornis roseicollis*).

**lovebirds
(*Agapornis
personata*).**

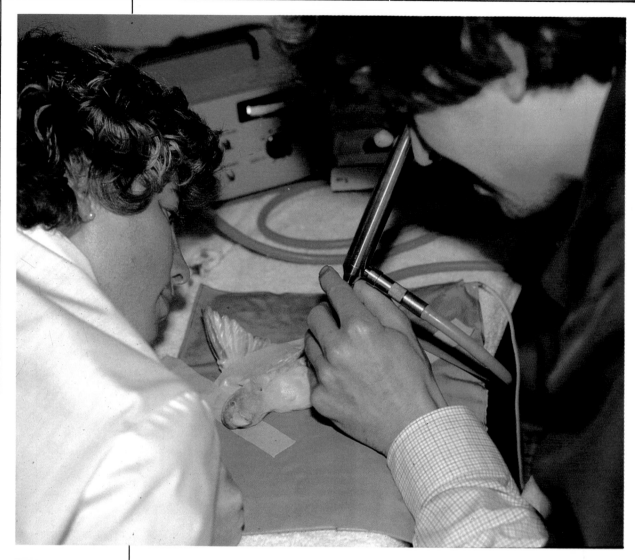

apparently loving "pair" for ages, only to discover that they have two cocks or two hens! In some species, there is no sexual dimorphism, which means the sexes are not visibly distinguishable by markings, color, size or form; in such cases, problems will arise in selecting true pairs. One way to overcome this is to acquire several birds of the same species, introduce them all into an aviary together with adequate nestboxes, and wait for them to pair up. Those birds which have not made a strong bond with another in a few days should be removed to separate accommodations. This method is, however, not wholly reliable,

nor always practicable, especially with some of the rarer mutations. Recently, surgical sexing, or laparotomy, has made it possible to sex lovebirds from the age of four months. This is achieved by anesthetizing the bird and inserting a probe through a small incision in its flank. You can find out where this can be carried out from your veterinarian. It is a reliable method of sex determination, but is somewhat drastic and stressful to the bird. Other methods of laboratory sex determination are now being researched, including hormonal examinations of the droppings of individual birds. In the future, sexing lovebirds may just be a case of keeping a bird alone in a cage until its droppings can be collected for examination.

Other methods of sexing non-dimorphic lovebirds are less reliable, although earlier breeders always seemed to get by one way or another. One method was to examine the bird's pelvic area, which is wider in breeding hens than in cocks. It is also said that the spread between the feet of the hen, when perching, is up to 1 cm (approximately 1/2 in) greater than that of the cock. Breeding behavior is of great significance in distinguishing the sexes. Only the hens carry nesting material,

so if both of a pair are performing this task, you are likely to have two hens. Conversely, total lack of breeding activity may indicate that you have two cocks!

NESTBOXES

Nestboxes should be available all year round, for the birds use them to roost in at night, even outside the breeding period. The birds should be discouraged from breeding during the colder months (unless they are kept indoors), as the chicks are likely to die in the shell or catch severe chills after hatching. Almost any form of compact cavity with an

"Nestboxes should be available all year round, for the birds use them to roost in at night, even outside the breeding period."

Masked lovebird (*Agapornis personata*).

*"It is wise to have
a spare nestbox for
each pair of birds
so that a clean box
can be
exchanged. . .for
the one in which
the birds have
been roosting."*

A normal green
peach-faced
lovebird
(*Agapornis
personata*).

entrance hole of about 5 cm (2 in) in diameter will be accepted by most species, but it is best to have the internal measurements be 15–17.5 cm (6–7 in) square at the base and 25 cm (10 in) high, with the entrance hole just below the roof. A short perch should be affixed just below the entrance

hole so the birds have somewhere to grip as they enter or leave the box. Nestboxes can be made from plywood, wooden planks or hollowed out logs. They should preferably have a rain-proof, sloping roof and an access door so that the nest may be examined in cases of emergency.

Boxes should be located in the shelter or under the covered part of the outside flight where the humidity is likely to be higher. Lovebirds require a fairly high level of humidity in the nest if the eggs are to develop satisfactorily. This can be helped by having a shallow pond or dish of water in the aviary where the birds can wet their feathers and carry moisture to the nest. It is wise to have a spare nestbox for each pair of birds so that a clean box can be exchanged (in the same position) for the one in which the birds have been roosting. This will ensure that the boxes are free of red mite or other parasites, which can severely handicap satisfactory development of the chicks. Large infestations will inhibit growth, cause anemia and may result in death, while irritation caused by parasites can result in feather plucking, a habit difficult to stop once it has started.

NESTING MATERIALS

Most lovebird species use nesting materials of some sort, and the nest itself may range from a shallow base to a complete dome. The Abyssinian lovebird, however, uses virtually

necked containers of water sunk into the aviary floor, so that they remain fresh and keep moist. Some birds will collect leaves and strips of bark and place them between their rump feathers to transport them to their nests, while others, particularly those of the white eyeringed group, will carry the material in their beaks.

BREEDING BEHAVIOR

A rich diet is required during

"Most lovebird species use nesting materials of some sort, and the nest itself may range from a shallow base to a complete dome."

no materials other than the rotting wood found in the base of a tree cavity. For this reason, it is best to provide a layer of slightly damp peat or sawdust in the bottom of the nestbox. Such a layer will not go amiss in the nestbox, as it will retain moisture and help keep humidity levels up. It is best to provide complete twigs from nonpoisonous trees such as apple, pear, cherry, hazel, willow, elder, etc. These can be placed upright in narrow-

the breeding period, so ensure that adequate food is available. Cuttlefish bone or other supplements containing calcium should be readily available during the season; hen birds will take increasing amounts as laying time approaches. Eggs are usually laid every second day, but serious incubation does not usually commence until after the second or third egg has been laid, thus bringing the chicks' hatching times to within a day or

A battery of lovebird breeding cages. Remember that lovebirds are usually more combative during the breeding season; therefore, they should only be kept one pair to a cage.

Above left: A nest of peach-faced lovebird (*Agapornis roseicollis*) eggs. Peach-faced lovebird clutches usually don't contain more than six eggs. *Above right:* Peach-faced nest with eggs and a newly hatched chick. *Below:* A three-week-old baby lovebird.

Left: Pastel blue and green cinnamon chicks. *Above:* Peach-faced chick prior to fledging. *Below:* Peach-faced chicks inside the nestbox.

*"During the
breeding period,
the birds are more
wary and, apart
from the
occasional
inspection of the
nest to ensure that
all is well. . .they
should be
disturbed as little
as possible."*

**Pied blue
peach-faced
lovebird
(*Agapornis
roseicollis*).**

two of each other. The hen does
all of the sitting, but the cock will
feed her and spend protracted
periods in the nestbox with her.
The incubation period is from
21–23 days, maybe a little
longer in cold weather. During
the breeding period, the birds
are more wary and, apart from
the occasional inspection of the
nest to ensure that all is well (do
this preferably when the birds
have left the nest to feed), they
should be disturbed as little as
possible. The size of the clutch
may range from one to nine
eggs, but is usually three or four.

The hatchlings are covered in a
soft down, the color depending
on the species. The first feather
quills will appear in a few days,
and fledging takes place in five
to seven weeks; all nestlings
from a brood usually hatch
within a period of 48 hours or
less. After fledging, the cock bird
will usually continue to feed the
young for a few days, but they

A peach-faced lovebird (*Agapornis roseicollis*) at the downy stage.

"The major problems which occur during breeding include French molt and egg-binding. The latter condition is potentially fatal and must be treated without delay."

A nearly clear pied blue peach-faced lovebird.

should soon start feeding themselves. During this time, one should keep a close watch for signs of aggression from the parents as, should they want to go to nest again, there is a danger that the hen will attack and seriously injure (or even kill) youngsters from the first brood if they are left in the same quarters. The youngsters should

be moved to a holding cage or aviary until one decides which are going to be kept for future breeding and which are to be sold.

BREEDING PROBLEMS

The major problems which occur during breeding include French molt and egg-binding. The latter condition is potentially fatal and must be treated without delay. An egg (or eggs) becomes lodged in the hen's ovary; and the bird will look sick, sitting in a sorry condition with its feathers fluffed out. This condition could be caused by several things, including a shortage of calcium, chilling and immaturity (lovebirds should not be bred until they are at least nine, preferably 12, months old). A bird suffering from egg-binding should be placed in a warm environment (hospital cage) and maintained at a temperature of 30°C (86°F). This alone is sufficient to alleviate the problem in the majority of cases, and the troublesome egg is successfully passed. In severe cases, a veterinarian should be consulted

Peach-faced lovebirds. Only birds that are in perfect condition should be bred.

Peach-faced lovebirds, a white and a lutino.

as soon as possible. An injection of calcium borogluconate will help relieve the disorder. Birds which suffer from egg-binding should not be bred again for at least a year.

Infertile eggs occur fairly frequently and can be caused by the birds' immaturity (or perhaps you just have two hens). Alternatively, chicks may die in the shell. This may be a result of dietary deficiencies in the hen, but is more likely to be caused by too low a degree of humidity in the nest chamber. This can occur in very dry seasons and, particularly, with members of the white eyering group being bred indoors. Facilities for the birds to bathe and an ample supply of fresh twigs, so that the hen can replenish the nest at regular intervals, should always be available.

Above: A gaggle of red-faced lovebirds (*Agapornis pullaria*). *Left:* Fischer's lovebird (*Agapornis fischeri*) egg compared with a cockatiel egg. The Fischer's egg is the smaller of the two.

Opposite: A pair of blue masked lovebirds (*Agapornis personata*) inside their domicile.

A clear pied green peach-faced lovebird (*Agapornis roseicollis*).

Black-cheeked lovebird (*Agapornis nigrigenis*).

"A mutation can be simply described as a change in the chromosome structure of an organism."

Normal green peach-faced lovebird.

COLOR BREEDING

Several lovebird species, the peach-faced in particular, can be described as being semi-domesticated. Domestication is a term which is applied to any animal that breeds through many generations in captivity, and in which strains of mutations and varieties are developed through selective breeding. A mutation can be simply described as a change in the chromosome structure of an organism. If this change occurs in a gamete (the specialized sex cell which combines with another gamete to produce a zygote, from which the next generation arises), the mutation is inherited by subsequent generations of offspring. In wild populations, mutations occur almost continuously, but only those which are favorable to the continuation of the species tend to survive. In captivity, such mutations can be exploited and

120

bred into future generations to give variations from the norm (usually variations in color, but variations in form are also possible). The mode of inheritance of mutations in lovebirds can be fitted into one of four simple groupings, based on the work of Gregor Mendel (1822–1884), who pioneered the study of genetics. The structures which control all the features of an individual (including color) are known as genes. These occur on the paired chromosomes, so that there are two genes for each characteristic, located on opposing chromosomes.

"The mode of inheritance in lovebirds can be fitted into one of four simple groupings, based on the work of Gregor Mendel. . .who pioneered the study of genetics."

Left: Yellow peach-faced lovebird. *Right:* Green cinnamon peach-faced lovebird.

The white peach-faced lovebird (*Agapornis roseicollis*) is produced by a cross of pastel blue and yellow factors.

"As the numbers of captive-bred offspring increase, the chances of a mutant appearing become more likely."

Normal green and American pied light green peach-faced lovebirds.

Autosomal Recessive Mutations: As the numbers of captive-bred offspring increase, the chances of a mutant appearing become more likely. In most cases, however, the normal coloration remains dominant and the mutation is referred to as recessive. If only one pair of genes becomes mutated, the bird will appear normal but will carry the mutated gene in its make-up. Such a bird is referred to as a normal "split" for whatever mutant is present. In Table 3 the normal and the pastel blue mutation of the peach-faced will be used to demonstrate the expected results of various pairings.

Green pied and
pastel blue
peach-faced
lovebirds.
Breeding
peach-faced
lovebirds
offers both
variety and
excitement for
more and more
hobbyists each
year.

The name "pastel
blue" is quite
troublesome to
many beginners
because it is not a
very accurate
description of the
true plumage
color, which is
really bluish-
green.

TABLE 3: Expected results from five possible pairings of normal and pastel blue peach-faced lovebirds.

1) Pastel Blue × Normal .... 100% Normal/Pastel Blue.
2) Pastel Blue × Normal/Pastel Blue .... 50% Pastel Blue
                                 + 50% Normal/Pastel Blue.
3) Pastel Blue × Pastel Blue .... 100% Pastel Blue.
4) Normal/Pastel Blue × Normal .... 50% Normal/Pastel Blue
                                 + 50% Normal
5) Normal/Pastel Blue × Normal/Pastel Blue .... 50% Normal/Pastel Blue
                                 + 25% Pastel Blue
                                 +25% Normal.

Sex-linked Recessive Mutations: The sex chromosomes in the male are of the same length, while in the female, one is shorter than the other. Sex-linked recessive chromosomes are confined exclusively to a pair of sex chromosomes, so it is impossible for a hen to be split for a mutation which occurs on the shorter chromosome, as there is no corresponding portion for the gene to be present. Peach-faced hens must be either lutino or normal; they cannot be normal/lutino (normal split for lutino) as is the case with cocks. Table 4 gives the expected results of experimental pairings.

The chicks will not always conform to the expected result, as these calculations are based on expectancies from large numbers of matings. The more chicks produced from a particular pair, the closer the results will be to the calculated expectations. It should not be assumed that a cock bird of normal appearance is not split for lutino if no lutinos appear among the chicks of a single clutch. However, the presence of a single lutino chick in a nest will confirm that the male parent is split, providing the hen is normal.

TABLE 4: Expected results from five possible pairings of normal and lutino peach-faced lovebirds.

1) Normal cock × Lutino hen .... 50% Normal/Lutino cocks
   + 50% Normal hens.

2) Normal/Lutino cock × Normal hen .... 25% Normal cocks
   + 25% Normal/Lutino cocks
   + 25% Normal hens
   + 25% Lutino hens

3) Normal/Lutino cock × Lutino hen .... 25% Normal/Lutino cocks
   + 25% Lutino cocks
   + 25% Normal hens
   + 25% Lutino hens

4) Lutino cock × Normal hen .... 50% Normal/Lutino cocks
   + 50% Lutino hens.

5) Lutino cock × Lutino hen .... 50% Lutino cocks
   + 50% Lutino hens.

American pied light green peach-faced lovebird. This variety is sometimes called the dilute yellow-green.

Dominant Mutations: The only mutation which is dominant to the normal in peach-faced lovebirds is the pied, and in this case a reversal of the autosomal recessive mutation exists. In this case, the mutant birds are known as single and double factor (s.f. and d.f. respectively), depending on whether one or both of a pair of genes are affected. Results to be expected from pied pairings are given in Table 5.

It is not possible to distinguish between single and double factor birds by appearance. However, if normals should result from a pairing of a pied with a normal, then the former must be a single factor bird.

Headstudy of a lutino peach-faced lovebird (*Agapornis roseicollis*).

TABLE 5: Expected results from five possible pairings of pied peach-faced lovebirds.

1) Pied (s.f.) × Normal .... 50% Pied + 50% Normal.
2) Pied (d.f.) × Normal .... 100% Pied.
3) Pied (s.f.) × Pied (s.f.) .... 50% Pied (s.f.)
   + 25% Pied (d.f.)
   + 25% Normal.
4) Pied (s.f.) × Pied (d.f.) .... 50% Pied (s.f.)
   + 50% Pied (d.f.)
5) Pied (d.f.) × Pied (d.f.) .... 100% Pied (d.f.)

A pastel blue or Dutch blue peach-faced lovebird.

Incomplete Dominant Mutations: It is possible to distinguish between single factor and double factor birds in this category on the basis that the latter are darker in color. The mutation modifies the color or shade, rather than the color itself. For peach-faced mutations, Table 6 gives a summary of expected results.

Above: A trio of yellow peach-faced lovebirds *(Agapornis roseicollis).* *Right:* Fischer's lovebird *(Agapornis fischeri)* and masked lovebird *(Agapornis personata).*

"The mutation modifies the color or shade, rather than the color itself."

TABLE 6: Expected results from five possible pairings of olive (d.f.), dark green (s.f.), and normal peach-faced lovebirds.

1) Olive (d.f.) × Olive (d.f.) .... 100% Olive (d.f.)
2) Olive (d.f.) × Dark Green (s.f.) .... 50% Olive (d.f.)
   + 50% Dark Green (s.f.)
3) Olive (d.f.) × Normal Green .... 100% Dark Green (s.f.)
4) Dark Green (s.f.) × Dark Green (s.f.) .... 50% Dark Green (s.f.)
   + 25% Normal Green
   + 25% Olive (d.f.).
5) Dark Green (s.f.) × Normal Green .... 50% Dark Green (s.f.)
   + 50% Normal Green.

A dark pastel blue or cobalt peach-faced lovebird.

Health and Hygiene

"Hygiene often sounds more complicated than it really is; all that is really required to keep birds in good health is thoughtful and thorough husbandry."

Health is a difficult word to define, but most people know what is meant by "good health" or "bad health." Obviously, if you keep lovebirds, you want to keep them in good health at all times, and you can go a long way towards this goal by practicing good standards of avicultural hygiene. Hygiene is the science, or art, of preserving good health (or preventing disease and bad health, whichever way you wish to interpret it). In keeping groups of birds under close confinement, hygiene is of utmost importance. Infectious diseases can spread very rapidly from one bird to the next unless strict and logical hygienic measures are taken. Hygiene often sounds more complicated than it really is; all that is really required to keep birds in good health is thoughtful and thorough husbandry. Provided with the correct nourishment and kept in clean, dry, draft-proof and vermin-free quarters, lovebirds should remain in good health and live to a ripe old age of ten years or even more.

An American pied light green peach-faced lovebird (*Agapornis roseicollis*). All healthy lovebirds should have bright eyes, tight clean plumage, and an alert, aware demeanor.

An American white peach-faced lovebird.

Fischer's lovebirds (*Agapornis fischeri*). Overcrowding creates an unhealthy, stressful situation for lovebirds. Be sure to provide roomy housing for your birds.

"The first rule of hygiene in aviculture is to be sure that the original and subsequent stock acquisitions are in good health at the outset."

CHOOSING STOCK

The first rule of hygiene in aviculture is to be sure that the original and subsequent stock acquisitions are in good health at the outset. Stock should be obtained only from approved dealers and breeders. Unclean or dubious premises should be avoided and, wherever possible, it is best to select and collect your own birds rather than have them delivered by mail or phone order, even if there is some kind of guarantee of their "live arrival." Select birds that are clean, alert, bright-eyed and full-colored, with tight, neat plumage. Never purchase birds with ruffled feathers, bald patches or those that sit moping in some corner showing little interest in what is going on. Handle the birds before purchase if possible, and give them a close examination. They can give quite a painful nip with their sharp and powerful little bills, so it may be wise to wear a leather glove. Birds in aviaries are usually caught up in a net with a padded rim, then transferred to the hand. If in a cage, a bird may be caught straight into the hand, but a little practice at this is required. Handle gently but firmly, gripping the whole body around the wings and restraining the head gently between the fingers. This will allow you to first examine the vent, which should be clean and have no signs of wetness or encrustations among the surrounding feathers. Next, unfurl the wings one at a time, and examine for deformities or injuries. Look at the eyes, nostrils and mouth for signs of discharges, and blow gently into the feathers to look for external parasites or skin blemishes. Having ascertained that the prospective purchase is apparently healthy, it may then be placed into an appropriate carrying box and transported home without delay. Most bird dealers provide specially made cartons which hold just one bird (it is always advisable to

"Having ascertained that the prospective purchase is apparently healthy, it may then be placed into an appropriate carrying box and transported home without delay."

Masked lovebird (*Agapornis personata*). As soon as you acquire your new pet, have your veterinarian, pet dealer, or an experienced aviculturist show you the proper way to handle a lovebird. Handling is a must when it comes to checking for parasites, for nail-clipping, and for sexing, to name just a few situations.

This page: A male Abyssinian lovebird (*Agapornis taranta*). It is important to place perches of different widths in the cage so that the gripping muscles of the feet are exercised. *Opposite:* Masked lovebird (*Agapornis personata*).

transport birds in individual compartments if possible). Do not be tempted to open the box "just for a quick look" during the journey; many new purchases are lost in this way! In addition, never leave birds in a cardboard box for too long, as they will soon gnaw their way out. On no account should birds be left in parked cars on a sunny day, for obvious reasons!

QUARANTINE

Should you already have birds at home, it is most important that new acquisitions undergo a period of quarantine before introducing them to existing stock. This quarantine is in addition to any which may have been carried out by the dealer under import regulations. Quarantine is a period of isolation in order to watch the new bird for any signs of developing disease, which may have been in its early, unrecognizable stages at the time of purchase but may

Lutino peach-faced lovebird (*Agapornis roseicollis*). The breast of a healthy lovebird should be plump and full.

develop into recognizable symptoms at a later stage. Quarantine accommodations, preferably cages, should be kept in a separate room, well away from existing stock. New birds should be kept in quarantine for a minimum of 14 days. Should any disease develop in this period, the bird should be treated and kept away from other stock until it is completely cured.

DISEASES AND TREATMENT

Lovebirds may be susceptible to a variety of diseases but, fortunately, these are exceptions rather than the rule in well-kept establishments. Should a bird become sick, however, it is wise to know what steps to take. An ailing bird will usually sit moping in a corner, or at the end of a perch, with its plumage fluffed out and, often, with its head tucked under its wing. It will lose its appetite, and its weight and condition will rapidly deteriorate. A characteristic "hollowing" of the normally plump breast region will be discernible in a bird which has been off its food for a few days. These symptoms occur in many kinds of diseases, some of which may be diagnosed by the appearance of other symptoms. Should you be unsure about the disease in question or its method of treatment, you are advised to consult a veterinarian. If your local vet is not experienced in avian diseases, he will most certainly be able to put you in touch with one who is.

A bird which is obviously sick should be immediately isolated from other stock and placed in a warm, dry, draft-proof situation, preferably in semi-darkness. Many ailing birds will quickly respond to quiet rest and heat

treatment. It will be an asset to have a hospital cage as part of one's equipment. Such a cage is covered with glass or plexiglass to prevent drafts and to retain heat. The heat source is in the base of the cage, and the temperature can be adjusted by setting a thermostat. The ailing bird is placed in the cage and the temperature is maintained at about 32°C (90°F). The favorite food of the bird should be placed in a container within easy reach of the perch, and fresh water should be available at all times.

Sick birds are usually reluctant to feed and, all too often, it is the effect of starvation which is fatal rather than the disease itself. Birds should therefore be encouraged to feed by offering them the choicest tidbits. A stubborn bird which continually refuses to feed must be hand-fed. A suitable mixture for producing energy and fighting disease can be made by mixing a teaspoon of honey or corn syrup into a cup of hot milk; then add a beaten egg yolk and a tiny pinch of salt. Mix this together thoroughly and allow to cool to lukewarm temperature. The mixture can be administered by picking the bird up in the hand

Masked lovebird (*Agapornis personata*). Occasionally, the beak of a lovebird may become overgrown if the bird is not getting enough gnawing exercise. Have an expert show you the proper way to trim the beak to a proper size.

139

A normal green peach-faced lovebird (*Agapornis roseicollis*).

and gently forcing the beak open with the fingers of the same hand. The mixture is fed drop by drop into the mouth by means of a small syringe or a glass eye dropper (which may be obtained from a drug store). Alternatively, the fluid can be dribbled into the bird's mouth from a teaspoon. Medicines prescribed by a veterinarian can also be administered in these ways.

Mechanical Injuries: These are fractures or wounds caused by fighting or flying into a window or cage wire after having

received a fright. Such injuries are fortunately uncommon, but if they should occur, the injured bird should be isolated and a veterinarian consulted. A fractured bone in the leg can be repaired with a small splint and adhesive plaster; wings may be set in position with adhesive tape alone. Splints should be left in position for seven or eight weeks to allow the fracture to heal. Flesh wounds should be bathed with a mild solution of antiseptic. In cases of heavy bleeding or extensive lacerations, a veterinarian should be consulted immediately.

Overgrown Claws and Beaks: Birds which have access to perches of varied diameters and twigs on which to keep their beaks in trim are unlikely to become afflicted with either of these problems. They may occasionally occur, however, and must be treated before they develop into a fatal situation. Overgrown nails can be simply trimmed down using sharp nail scissors or clippers. The toes should be held up to the light so that the quick or blood supply to the nail can be seen. Great care must be taken to ensure that the quick is not severed during clipping, as profuse bleeding will occur. If this should happen accidentally, the bleeding should be stopped as soon as possible, using a styptic pencil or some alum. An overgrown beak can be a major problem, as the bird will be unable to feed properly and will starve if left untreated. The beak can be trimmed back as near as possible to a normal shape using nail clippers. If you should accidentally cut into the blood supply while doing this, the same treatment as for bleeding nails should be administered.

"Despite much research into the problem, the cause or the treatment of French molt is little understood; it seems to happen among some stock but not among other, apparently similar stock."

French Molt: Despite much research into the problem, the cause or the treatment of French molt is little understood; it seems to happen among some stock but not among other, apparently similar stock. Fledging birds suffering from this condition lose their tail and flight feathers and are thus unable to fly. Such birds are commonly referred to as "runners" or "infantrymen." Less severely affected birds will eventually regrow their feathers; in some cases, however, the feathers remain missing. These birds are best painlessly destroyed.

Eye Disorders: Eye infections may be brought on by cold drafts, so good, draft-proof sleeping quarters are required. Eye disorders are usually heralded by watery or yellowish discharges, accompanied by inflammation and reddening of the eyelids. In many cases the bird will sit with its eyes half-shut. Most eye infections respond readily to an application of antiseptic or antibiotic eye ointments available on consultation with your vet.

American pied light green peach-faced lovebird.

141

Normal green peach-faced lovebirds (*Agapornis roseicollis*).

"Birds suffering from stress due to being kept in drafty, damp conditions are most susceptible to respiratory disorders."

Enteric Diseases: Infectious disorders in the digestive system are frequently referred to as "enteritis." There are a number of such conditions with a variety of causes, ranging from unsuitable diet (too much greenfood, for example) to infections of various parts of the alimentary canal by bacteria, protozoa or viruses. Crop trouble, in which the crop fills with frothy gas and becomes bloated, sometimes occurs in lovebirds. The bird will retch and vomit and the feathers will become stained. To treat this condition, hold the bird head downwards and gently "milk" out the crop. This disorder can be avoided by adding a little potassium permanganate to the drinking water, just enough to add a slight tinge of pink. Intestinal enteritis is heralded by the bird having an exceedingly poor appearance and by the presence of diarrhea. The feces may be greenish or watery, and the bird will lose its appetite. Infected birds should be isolated in a hospital cage and a veterinarian consulted. Diagnosis of the disease can usually be accomplished by laboratory examination of a fecal sample. Many such diseases are successfully treated with antibiotics.

Respiratory Infections: Labored breathing and a discharge from the beak and nostrils are signs of respiratory infections. These include infections of the upper respiratory tract, which, if left untreated, can develop into fatal pneumonia or infection of the air sacs. Birds suffering from stress due to being kept in drafty, damp conditions are most susceptible to respiratory disorders. Infected birds should be isolated in a hospital cage, and treatment should be carried out as recommended by a veterinarian.

A beautiful healthy normal green peach-faced lovebird. The feet and the head should be checked regularly for any signs of mites or other external parasites.

A lutino peach-faced lovebird (*Agapornis roseicollis*).

An American pied Dutch blue peach-faced lovebird.

Above: A blue masked lovebird (*Agapornis personata*). Check any and all food for freshness before giving it to your bird; if you don't you could wind up with a very sick pet. *Opposite:* A blue masked lovebird showing the results of feather plucking.

An olive peach-faced lovebird (*Agapornis roseicollis*). This color is produced by a double dark factor.

External Parasites: There are a number of bloodsucking organisms which may cause problems in a stock of lovebirds. Red mite, *Dermanyssus gallinae*, is quite common and may be introduced into aviaries by wild birds. In the daytime, the mites usually hide in cracks or dark corners of the aviary, or in nestboxes, crawling onto the birds at night to feed on their blood. Severe infestations will cause irritation, loss of rest, and anemia. Fortunately, red mite can be easily controlled by using one of the excellent miticides available from avicultural suppliers; follow the manufacturer's instructions. Bird lice of various kinds may also pose a problem, but these, again, may be controlled by using special insecticides. Regular cleaning and disinfection of cages, aviaries and other accessories, particularly at the end of the breeding season, will help keep a check on external parasites.

Internal Parasites: These are organisms which live inside a bird's body and make a living at the expense of the bird. Those that cause major problems include roundworms, threadworms and tapeworms. These live in the bird's intestines and feed on partially digested food; severe infestations can deny the bird sufficient nutrients, and it will therefore rapidly lose condition. The worms' eggs are passed out in the feces of an infected bird and, if they find their way into foodstuffs, they will continually re-infect the stock. Infections can be kept under control by strict hygienic procedures, particularly with regard to feeding. Regular microscopic examinations of fecal samples in a veterinary laboratory may reveal the presence of worm eggs. There are various anthelminthic (worming) compounds available; they should always be used to the manufacturer's instructions. After severe worm infections, the cage or aviary should be thoroughly disinfected and the topsoil in outside flights should be changed in order to remove any surviving eggs.

Normal green peach-faced lovebird. Most expert breeders do not let their exhibition charges have free-flying freedom, as too many accidents can occur.

Exhibiting Lovebirds

A prize-winning female Abyssinian lovebird (*Agapornis taranta*) resting in her cage after a tough day at the show.

At some time or other, most aviculturists have a desire to exhibit their breeding successes by entering them into competition with birds produced by other breeders. These exhibitions are usually organized by specific or general avicultural societies, a number of which exist in most countries. It is highly recommended that any lovebird enthusiast join such a society, from which he can considerably enrich his knowledge of the hobby by discussing strategies with fellow enthusiasts, and by reading the newsletters giving details of the successes (and failures) of other breeders, thereby preparing himself for success on the show bench.

PREPARING FOR A SHOW

Unless trained from a very young age, lovebirds do not make good exhibition birds, as they are naturally nervous and sit cooped up in a corner of the show cage looking sorry for themselves. The most suitable birds are usually produced by selective breeding—that is, by pairing the best cock of a particular type to the best hen and hoping that the desirable points of each are reproduced in the offspring. Unfortunately,

"Unless trained from a very young age, lovebirds do not make good exhibition birds, as they are naturally nervous and sit cooped up in a corner of the cage looking sorry for themselves."

Male Madagascar lovebird (*Agapornis cana*).

"...it is futile to enter a bird with a bald patch or a toe missing in the hope that its other attributes will make it a winner."

undesirable characteristics, which may not have been noticed in the parents, may be doubly apparent in the young. It can therefore be a bit of a hit-and-miss affair for several generations until ideal show specimens are produced. Another problem which arises is that birds earmarked for exhibition cannot, at the same time, be used for breeding. It would be a rather drastic decision to remove a member of a breeding pair in the middle of the breeding season for exhibition purposes. Young birds should therefore be selected almost as soon as they have left the nest. They should be regularly placed in small show-type cages and accustomed to being peered at from close proximity. Although lovebirds are normally exhibited in pairs, should one of a pair be out of condition, it is usually acceptable

to exhibit a single bird so that there is at least a chance to gain a few valuable merit points. In the case of sexually dimorphic species, it is usually obligatory to exhibit a cock and a hen.

Only birds in immaculate condition should be entered for exhibition; it is futile to enter a bird with a bald patch or a toe missing in the hope that its other attributes will make it a winner. All exhibition birds should have perfect plumage and color, should be robust in shape and have no physical deformities. All toenails should be present and of appropriate length, and the beak should not be distorted.

SHOW CAGES

At present, there appear to be no particular standards laid down for lovebird show cages, but the type used for budgerigars are often recommended. A show cage is a rectangular boxlike structure with a wire front and a small access door in one of its ends. The outside and inside of the cage are painted with non-toxic gloss paint, usually in black and white respectively. Two perches are set near either end, about halfway up the back wall and not quite reaching the wire front. Water and food hoppers are placed in special spaces in the lower front of the cage. Cages used for exhibition must be in perfect condition, and it is best to thoroughly prepare them just a couple of days before the show so that they do not become scratched or soiled.

ENTERING THE SHOW

One should be familiar with exhibition procedures before actually entering a bird in a show. It is a good idea to attend as many shows as possible to study from. Try to have a word with the secretary and one or two judges (but, not while judging is in progress!) they will usually be pleased to give you advice and answer any specific questions.

Before entering birds in a show, obtain a schedule of the classes from the secretary as early as possible. Complete the entry form and submit it in good time, as entries are seldom accepted after the closing date. Do not be disappointed if your birds are unsuccessful the first time you exhibit—this is not unusual! Each time you exhibit birds, you will be gaining more experience in what the judges are looking for, and you will be able to go away and improve your stock for next time. Once you have a winning strain and you know how to maintain it in prime condition, there is no reason why you should not continue to take prizes time and time again.

"Each time you exhibit birds, you will be gaining more experience in what the judges are looking for, and you will be able to go away and improve your stock for next time."

A pair of Fischer's lovebirds (*Agapornis fischeri*). Exhibition birds cannot be bred during the show season. This fact is just plain common sense, as breeding takes a lot of stamina and, therefore, usually detracts from the bird's appearance.

Dutch blue ino peach-faced lovebird (*Agapornis roseicollis*).

Lutino peach-faced lovebird.

Suggested Reading

Partial contents of Breeding Lovebirds:
Introduction ●
Captive Breeding ●
Species of Lovebirds ●
Availability ●
General Maintenance ●
Breeding Lovebirds ●
Diseases

BREEDING LOVEBIRDS
by Tony Silva and Barbara Kotlar
ISBN 0-86622-722-9
TFH KW-125

This book, illustrated with 80 full-color photographs, presents sensible, easy-to-follow recommendations about all aspects of caring for and breeding lovebirds. It concentrates on providing readers with all the information they need and want in an interesting and easy-to-read style.

THE COMPLETE CAGE AND AVIARY BIRD HANDBOOK
by David Alderton
ISBN 0-86622-113-1
TFH H-1087

Author David Alderton, well-known for his books and articles on avicultural subjects, examines the whole field of cage and aviary birds. Treating the species by family, he provides current up-to-date information on both the popular species and many of the less commonly seen birds as well. Full-color illustrations help the reader identify the species and varieties along with excellently detailed illustrations showing the design of aviaries and furnishings.

THE COMPLETE BIRDS OF THE WORLD (ILLUSTRATED EDITION)
by Michael Walters
ISBN 0-87666-894-5
TFH H-1022

This book lists every bird species in the world and gives for each the family relationship, range, common and scientific names, and related important data. Birds of 120 different families are shown in beautiful full-color photos; there are more than 550 full-color illustrations in total. This magnificent volume enables bird watchers, aviculturists, dealers, and scientists to learn the distribution, habitat, feeding and nesting habits, clutch size, incubation and fledgling period of every family of birds in existence. Written by one of the world's foremost bird authorities and illustrated with some of the finest natural history photographs ever published, this immensely colorful and useful book will be referred to for years regardless of where in the world the reader may live. This volume is fully indexed with both common and scientific names for easy reference. A treasure to own and a pleasure to show, it is one of the finest ornithological works ever produced.

PARROTS OF THE WORLD
by Joseph M. Forshaw
ISBN 0-87666-959-3
TFH PS-753

This book covers every species and subspecies of parrot in the world, including those recently extinct. Information is presented on distribution, habitat, status, and general habits. Almost 500 species and subspecies are illustrated in full-color. This remarkable and beautiful book, valued almost as much for its sheer looks as for its highly valuable information, is a delight to parrot lovers and book lovers alike.

THE WORLD OF LOVEBIRDS
by Jürgen Brockmann and Werner Lantermann
ISBN 0-86622-927-2
TFH H-1092

Besides complete coverage of the principal aspects of lovebird keeping, this work devotes special attention to the breeding of color varieties. The known color varieties found in each species are treated in detail, based on the models developed in connection with the many varieties developed in the peach-faced lovebird (*Agapornis roseicollis*). Contains over 70 full-color photographs and many black-and-white drawings.

PARROTS AND RELATED BIRDS
by Henry J. Bates and Robert L. Busenbark
ISBN 0-87666-967-4 new edition
TFH H-912

This is the "bible" for parrot lovers. It has more color photographs and more information on parrots than any other single book on the subject. The latest edition has recently been updated with new information and color photographs. Written primarily for the owner of more than one parrot or parrot-like bird, this is a necessary reference work for libraries, pet shops, and airport officials who most identify imported birds.

ENCYCLOPEDIA OF PARAKEETS
by Kurt Kotlar and Karl Heinz Spitzer
ISBN 0-86622-926-4
TFH H-1094

This book covers the long-tailed members of the parrot family generally in their housing, dietary, breeding, and health needs. The thorough coverage ranges from little-known species like the night parakeet to the familiar budgerigar and cockatiel. Species accounts constitute the main portion of the text, with worldwide coverage—the Americas, Africa, Australia, and the islands of the Pacific.

Partial contents of The World of Lovebirds: Lovebirds, Our Favorite Small Parrots ● Their Homeland and Life in the Wild ● Accommodations, Diet, and Illness ● Lovebirds as Tame Household Companions? ● Behavior Patterns of Lovebirds ● Breeding Lovebirds ● The Species of Lovebirds ● Color Varieties and Their Inheritance

TAMING AND TRAINING LOVEBIRDS
by Risa Teitler
ISBN 0-86622-986-8
TFH KW-038

Well-known bird trainer Risa Teitler gives thorough, easy-to-understand methods for taming and training the pet lovebird. In the author's own words, this book is "intended as a guide for those who desire to own a tame pet lovebird. . .If you follow the suggestions given, you should be able to show off your tame pet in a short time." This volume is completely illustrated with full-color photography.

BIRD DISEASES: AN INTRODUCTION TO THE STUDY OF BIRDS IN HEALTH AND DISEASE
by Drs. L. Arnall and I.F. Keymer
ISBN 0-87666-950-X
TFH H-964

This is a highly specialized book written for bird pathologists and dealers. Experienced bird lovers can recognize symptoms and diseases from the many illustrations and thus will be able to treat their own birds since "bird doctors" are so few and far between.

A pair of Dutch blue ino peach-faced lovebirds (*Agapornis roseicollis*).

A pair of masked lovebirds (*Agapornis personata*).

Index

**Pastel blue
peach-faced
lovebird
(Agapornis
roseicollis).**